HOW TO HAVE AN ADVENTURE IN
SCOTLAND
RAFFAEL CORONELLI

By Raffael Coronelli

How to Have an Adventure in Scotland

ISBN: 9798713931056

First Edition: April 2021

Dedicated to all my friends in Scotland.

Glasgow

Arrival in Glasgow
A Hardman's City

"This is your captain, Ian Fleming."

Well then, that's certainly a way to begin a trip to the British Isles. Seated in the British Airways jumbo jet and ready for the seven-hour transatlantic flight from Chicago, I'd be flown by Ian Fleming himself — or at least a qualified British airline captain who shared his name. You can't make this stuff up.

The flight itself is nothing. I've had thirteen-hour flights to Japan. At least on a nonstop half-day to Asia, though, you can get a full night's sleep. On a flight to Europe, you really just get a five hour nap between settling in your seat and waking up to breakfast. At least the food and drink service on a transatlantic British Airways flight is good.

An amicable flight attendant served me a tiny bottle of Glenlivet Scotch — a nice rich single-malt that whet my appetite for the smorgasbord of delightful whiskies to come. I was headed to the best place on Earth to taste Scotches.

I'll be getting fairly specific about my sampling and recommendation of Scotch whiskies. I've compiled a handy list and included it at the back of the book for reference when you find yourself in a Scottish pub. We'll get to that type of scenario later.

Glenlivet was perfect to sip while drifting into a nap watching the 1925 silent film adaptation of Arthur Conan Doyle's *The Lost World* on the seat-back screen as I looked forward to the adventure ahead. I was embarking on a journey that would take me through highland medieval castles, abyssal lochs, primordial landscapes emerging from the mists of time.

RAFFAEL CORONELLI

A quick layover at Heathrow allowed me just enough time to pass through customs and catch my flight north. England passed below, the hills of Yorkshire rolling away as we zipped across the English border and into the Scottish lowlands. Thick fog enveloped the plane as it descended. Then, the fog broke, and I saw the city.

Victorian architecture and dark alleyways greeted me from below, a city whose culture I could feel even before touching the low road before us. There was only one place in the world in which I could possibly be.

HOW TO HAVE AN ADVENTURE IN
SCOTLAND
RAFFAEL CORONELLI

RAFFAEL CORONELLI

The reason for the timing of my trip was to attend the wedding of my Scottish friend, Steven. What I could've done was seen Glasgow for a day or so, then gone to the wedding and gone home. Instead, I'd planned a two and a half week excursion across Scotland, from Glasgow to Stirling, then up into the highlands before coming back down to Edinburgh.

I might as well, I thought, since the single most expensive part of a trip is usually the airfare to get there if you plan well enough. Once you've reached your exotic overseas locale, I always recommend making the most of it that your schedule allows.

Past the terminal's baggage claim, I recognized a familiar face. Steven had come to the airport to meet me as soon as I'd arrived, which was actually a surprise. Considering he'd be getting married in two days, it was more than I would've ever expected, but that was just the level of hospitality for which I was in store.

Hopping on the bus in to the city, we chatted and caught up. Steven and I were both in our mid twenties and had been friends for years after meeting at a convention stateside. I remarked that looking out the front of the bus in the UK is always a little alarming, since it's on the opposite side of the road from what I was used to in the US. Around us, Victorian style buildings grew more dense. Soon, we were in the heart of Glasgow.

I'd be staying at an airbnb in the Merchant City neighborhood near George Square, the center of the city.

HOW TO HAVE AN ADVENTURE IN SCOTLAND

George Square

George Square is magnificent, surrounded by towering edifices of the Victorian era architecture for which Glasgow is known. Among them is the city hall, which looks a little bit like a castle — an appetizer for the ones I'd be seeing on my Scottish journey.

Steven recalled how there'd been a party in George Square on the night of the Scotland Independence Referendum in 2016 — which had ended without cause for the celebration.

"Maybe there'll be another one," I remarked.

He replied that there might if Brexit went through.

RAFFAEL CORONELLI

My trip to Scotland was in March of 2019 — months before Brexit finally occurred, and a full year before the unprecedented Coronavirus pandemic ravaged civilization. The United Kingdom and the world were entering a tumultuous period of time, but what exactly that would entail remained relatively uncertain for the time being.

Wandering through the streets of Glasgow's city center while we waited for my check-in time, Steven first took me to Buchanan Street. This pedestrian-only street is full of lovely shops and pubs. There was even a Tardis — or more accurately, an old fashioned police call box, now only used for decoration.

Passing a pub with an old sign reading "Cranston House," we decided to go in.

The pub itself was called Sloan's, and had a large outdoor seating area in a small alleyway courtyard with tables situated under decorative fairy lights. Inside, it had a homey atmosphere that I'd come to see is typical of pubs in Scotland.

Pulling up to the bar with my suitcase, I motioned to the bartender.

HOW TO HAVE AN ADVENTURE IN SCOTLAND

"I just got to Glasgow about half an hour ago," I grinned to him, a 20-something man who appeared immediately amused by my Chicago accent. "What should I drink?"

"Well," he thought for a moment. "St. Mungo?"

"Sounds good!" I replied.

The beer was excellent, a local lager named for the patron saint of Glasgow. It was an authentic Scottish beer experience, perfect for my first drink in the city.

Strings of lights hanging overhead, we sat in the alleyway outside the pub and enjoyed our drinks. Being outside in Glasgow is fantastic, because you're surrounded by incredible architecture and atmosphere. We left it at one pint each, leaving room for the evening to come before continuing our tour of the area.

Above: Sloan's outdoor courtyard

Right: A mural depicting St. Mungo in modern Glasgow

RAFFAEL CORONELLI

At the end of Ingram Street, we saw one of the primary landmarks of Glasgow — the Equestrian Statue of the First Duke of Wellington. Situated just outside the Gallery of Modern Art, this statue of the 19th century Duke on horseback is made notable by the way Glasgow citizens leave orange traffic cones on his head. Never have I seen the statue not wearing a traffic cone. It's become a symbol of Glaswegian culture and the city's cheeky sense of humor.

**The Equestrian Statue of the First Duke of Wellington
— with headwear**

HOW TO HAVE AN ADVENTURE IN SCOTLAND

Following the winding streets of Merchant City, we ended up at the apartment complex at which I'd be staying. The airbnb was essentially half of an apartment separated by a hallway. The other half was occupied by the airbnb's owner. I had my own bathroom and would be spending most of my time out and about anyway.

As a gift, Steven gave me a bottle of Famous Grouse's Bourbon Barrel Cask Series.

"I'm coming to your wedding, and you're giving me a gift?" I joked.

That was Scottish hospitality — or, maybe I just have the right friends there.

Drinking it over the next few months when I got home, it had a nice, woody flavor. I like Famous Grouse's standard blend well enough for an affordable option that's available everywhere, but this was from a special series — and a wonderful gift, of course. I'd have to keep it securely packed in with my clothes in my suitcase to prevent it from breaking. I recommend doing the same, since you'll no doubt want to come back from Scotland with a bottle of Scotch.

Situated in my accommodations, it was time to hit the town. I was lucky Steven was there, because having a local with you is the absolute best way to experience any city. You may or may not, so I'll give you a rundown of all the great places at which I found myself on that eventful night.

We were on our way to meet with another friend of ours, who lived in Glasgow proper working for a tour company as a guide.

Leaving Merchant City, we found ourselves at The Butterfly and the Pig — a chic, fashionable, but still authentically traditional pub. For my first real meal in Scotland, I decided to have a steak pie — a Scottish classic. It was delicious, a rich and savory way to fill myself up and brace my insides for the alcohol I was consuming.

"Steven," I asked, "since I'm the token foreigner at your wedding, are you gonna put me in the big wicker guy and light me on fire?"

"We were trying to keep that a secret," he answered coyly, prompting us all to laugh.

Our friend, a professional tour guide, asked me about my plans for the rest of the trip.

"I'm going all over," I explained. "Callander, for the wedding of course, and then Stirling, Inverness, Edinburgh."

"What are you doing in Inverness?"

"A few things. I've signed up for a tour of Loch Ness."

"What company?"

"Rabbies."

"Ah, they're great."

"Awesome, that's good to hear. When I found them I thought they were —"

"Rabies?" they laughed. "Yeah, it looks like 'rabies.'"

"Can't wait to get rabies from Nessie!" I added.

Finished with dinner and the sun beginning to set, it was time to move on to the night's activity — more pubs.

Glasgow has a lot of pubs, and they knew exactly which ones to take a first time visitor. To get to Hillhead, where the concentration of what they considered the best pubs was located, we'd need to take Glasgow's extremely limited subway.

I say limited, because Glasgow's subway is essentially one small loop that goes between a handful of neighborhoods. The city was an early adopter of the subway invention, but it never expanded beyond its initial route. I'm not even sure why it runs in two directions, since all it does is loop around. It's efficiently run and inexpensive, although it stops running at 6pm on Sundays.

That said, the subway got us to where we were headed quickly and effectively, and soon we were in the hopping West End neighborhood outside Hillhead station.

HOW TO HAVE AN ADVENTURE IN SCOTLAND

Left:
Hillhead Bookclub

Our first stop was the Hillhead Bookclub, a two-story pub with an upper lounge area. We got our drinks and sat up on the balcony on comfortable couches amidst vintage early 20th century decor. The Bookclub's architecture comes from the fact that it's situated in a former movie palace — arching, decorated ceiling and all. While the moviegoing experience is gone from the premises, it makes a unique setting for a bar.

When it came time to close out our tabs, I tipped the bartender two pounds, which seemed to take him aback. Tipping isn't as necessary in the UK as it is in the US, but you should still do it to avoid coming across as greedy. It's not like Japan, where tipping is considered an insult to the server and infers that they're not making a full wage; but it's not like the US, where the server will starve in front of you if you don't tip adequately. The guy seemed more than happy with his two pounds, but it made me realize that it might have been excessive.

Speaking of inventive locations for a pub, our next locale was down the street at Oran Mor — a great stone building dating to the mid-19th century. Initially a church, the castle-like tower is now a music venue with a pub in the basement. The towering spire, lit up at night with colorful spotlights, makes it impossible to miss. Inside, the stone walls and traditional decor make you feel like you're in some kind of medieval setting. Oran Mor is my personal favorite pub in Glasgow for the ambiance alone.

For our fifth pub of the day, and final stop of the night, we went to the Grosvenor. This big, brightly lit ballroom style establishment has a bar at the center, meaning that you sit along the edges of the room. It's an interesting layout, and I honestly have very little recollection of it since my hosts had been gracious enough to take me to four other bars prior to my arrival there.

This was pure Scottish hospitality, and my friends made sure I felt as welcome as possible. The amazing night eventually had to end, but I'd be seeing the lads in a couple days, in a different place. I said farewell for the time being, and slunk back on the subway to Merchant City.

HOW TO HAVE AN ADVENTURE IN SCOTLAND

Oran Mor

Tollbooth Steeple at Glasgow Cross

Sightseeing Glasgow
Gothic Splendor

I belong to Glasgow!
Dear old Glasgow town!
This song, sung for much of the previous night, gave me a suitable ear worm for my day of exploration.

Our friend's tour company, Glasgow City Sightseeing, had a bus leaving from George Square at noon. This would be a perfect way to get out to the city's various neighborhoods that aren't reachable via the subway. Until noon, I'd be left to my own devices in the city.

Heading to Buchanan Street for breakfast, I stopped into Cafe Nero — a coffee and tea chain that's essentially like Starbucks, but modeled after an Italian espresso cafe. As I got my coffee and a croissant to hold me over until lunch, I sat down on a couch next to the window.

Almost immediately, a woman sat down across from me with her small dog. She looked to be about in her mid 20's, but had a wild aura about her — something unhinged in her eyes.

"Hi!" I said enthusiastically in my American accent, the first explicit sign I wasn't a local.

"Hi," she laughed back. "You here for school?"

"No," I smiled. "I'm here for my friend's wedding."

"Oh, very good," she said. "You're from America?"

"Yeah, Chicago," I continued the conversation, taking a sip of my latte.

Scotland is not known for coffee. What you're going to end up with is usually either powdered instant coffee or espresso in water, so you might as well go for a fancier drink like a latte — or, just have tea.

"Do they support Ronald Reagan there?" she asked in her thick Scots accent.

I nearly spit out my drink at the bizarre and hilarious question. I almost wanted to ask if she supported Margaret Thatcher.

"Uh..." I stumbled, trying to think of a response. "No, he's dead."

"Oh, I see!" the manic look in her eyes grew wilder. "I've grown to love capitalism. I embrace capitalism!"

"That's nice," I said, shoving the entire croissant into my face and downing my coffee.

What proceeded to come out of her mouth was unintelligible, but definitely perturbed. Scots English is really a different language, a dialect of English with its own set of words and phrases that don't descend from the version spoken in England or the US, but rather ancient Gaelic roots.

I figured that, in this particular instance, not understanding her was fine. Most Scottish people I've met are lovely, but there are weirdos everywhere.

"That's super interesting," I purposely thickened my own Chicago accent while standing up and putting my coat on. "I gotta go meet up with some people, so, see ya."

"See ya!" said the strange woman.

Leaving Cafe Nero, I messaged my Scottish friends about the bizarre and uncomfortable encounter.

Uhhh that's f***in' wild, my Glaswegian friend replied. *But that lady does not represent the discussion style of most of us.*

HOW TO HAVE AN ADVENTURE IN SCOTLAND

In light of that, they'd encouraged me to try my first taste of Irn Bru, so I stopped into a Tesco convenience store to buy one.

Irn Bru is an orange soft drink — but it doesn't really taste like orange. I can't describe the taste other than sweet, refreshing, invigorating. I imagine it being drawn out of the Earth beneath Scotland, a wellspring from before the dawn of time. It's great, and instantly became my favorite soft drink in the world (possibly second only to Japan's Pocari Sweat, depending on what type of mood I'm in.)

Cracking open my Irn Bru, I wandered through the streets of Glasgow toward the river. This city bustled in early morning, people on their way to work hurrying between the buildings — and what interesting buildings they are.

I've mentioned the Victorian architecture of Glasgow, but it is incredibly striking just how much that aesthetic dominates the city. Out of all the places I've visited in the UK, Glasgow is the city with the most unified architectural vibe. Perhaps London would've shared the aesthetic if that city hadn't experienced the Blitz, but Glasgow's streets feel totally preserved from the Victorian era. It's a magnificent feeling, standing by the river and taking in the gothic splendor of it all.

Glasgow Royal Infirmary

Glasgow Bridge

After walking down to the River Clyde and finishing my Irn Bru, I stopped into The Briggait, an art gallery type space. Glasgow is a vibrant city full of art and culture, stemming from its large population of young people. The combination of nineteenth century architecture and modern art is a wonderful clash of aesthetics that I enjoyed taking in.

The Briggait

HOW TO HAVE AN ADVENTURE IN SCOTLAND

Noon approached, so I headed back up to George Square to look for the bus.

I fully understand the irony of this book being entitled *How to Have an Adventure*, and here I am telling you about how I got on a tour bus. How daring! How dangerous! Well, you try getting around the sprawling city of Glasgow entirely on your own, with a day to cover the sights and a subway system that only goes in a circle to the pubs and back.

In this instance, a bus tour is absolutely the best option to see most of the city in one fell swoop. Then, you can go through and see closer bits you find interesting after your introduction. You can even hop on and off the bus as it reaches various attractions, though I'd been planning on seeing the cathedral afterward, and that would take up my afternoon on its own. Feel free to plan accordingly, or just jump off the bus at any point you like (preferably after it stops moving). It is, after all, supposed to be an adventure.

Adventurously stepping up to the Glasgow City Sightseeing bus at the corner of George Square, I watched other tourists give their tickets to the driver.

Informing him that I was the friend of whom they'd been informed, he waved me into the bus without so much as a second thought.

Do not try this. Buy a ticket and go on the tour — it's inexpensive and well worth the price to get a comprehensive overview of the city's more disparate attractions.

I won't go into the list of all the sights the tour covers, because you can get that information on the tour itself. Dark, gothic streets rolling by the open top of the double-decker bus, cool wind blowing through my hair, I took in Glasgow from above. It was a magnificent vantage point to a magnificent city.

The bus covers a surprising amount of area, taking you down the river, past the main downtown district, all the way to the Glasgow Green and back. The guide frequently reminds you that city museums are free, so if you have time, you should take advantage of that. It's a wonderful thing for a city's museums' collections and knowledge to be available to the public free of charge.

Cemetery at Glasgow Cathedral

HOW TO HAVE AN ADVENTURE IN SCOTLAND

Back at George Square, I disembarked and began walking uphill in the direction of one of the sights we'd only passed on the tour — Glasgow Cathedral.

The cathedral is massive, but what's really striking about it is how it so embodies gothic architecture. As I made my way to the entrance, I looked up at the hillside cemetery silhouetted in the background, shrouded in mist. It felt like I was in a period horror film.

Glasgow Cathedral

RAFFAEL CORONELLI

Inside the cathedral, its cavernous decorum envelops you. Dark, intricately decorated, covered in fascinating reliefs, it completely fits the personality of the city for which it's named.

Glasgow Cathedral interior

Provand's Lordship

Nearby the cathedral is Provand's Lordship, a 15th century building constructed initially as part of the hospital, then converted into a home owned by the lord of the Provand in the early 19th century. Today, it's a medieval historical museum and serves as a remarkably immersive way to transport yourself back in time nearly half a millennium. It was one of my favorite attractions I visited in Glasgow.

RAFFAEL CORONELLI

I spent the remainder of the afternoon lost.
Wandering uphill from Provand's Lordship, I found myself
in the vicinity of Glasgow University. Tower blocks
surrounded me, and I realized I was in a neighborhood not
quite suited to sightseeing. Glasgow does have some
violence, but you'll probably be fine if you keep your wits
about you. Eventually I made my way to the hospital, and
then to the river. From there, I found my way back to George
Square in time to have dinner at a pub.

My pub of choice that evening, which I attended on
my own, was the Piper Whisky Bar. If you're a scotch lover
like me, then you absolutely have to go to the Piper while
you're in Glasgow. Their selection is second to none, and it's
all priced at a reasonable level that you can only find in
Scotland.

The pricing of scotch in Scotland is the most shocking
part of the experience. Scotch is renowned the world over,
but a 12 year aged single-malt will set you back more than is
considered a casual drinking price. In its home country,
though, you don't have to worry about breaking the bank.
Drink locally, and you'll be rewarded with fantastic tastes at
reasonable prices.

Stepping up to the bar at the Piper, I ordered a
Glenfiddich. The bar tender, a man about my age in his late
20's or early 30's, asked me to say it again.

"Glenfiddich," I repeated.

"I'm sorry," he said. "Let me go ask."

The bottle of Glenfiddich was right behind him —
which his coworker quickly pointed out.

"Sorry," he laughed, embarrassed, "it's your accent."

That was a first! For this Scottish bar tender, my
Chicago accent was just too intense and my pronunciation of
Glenfiddich was too far off the mark. I wasn't bothered at all,
it was just amusing. No matter, I got my scotch and a
delicious plate of bangers and mash.

HOW TO HAVE AN ADVENTURE IN SCOTLAND

My dinner was made even more pleasant by the atmosphere of the Piper — a real Scottish pub with friendly chatter and warm traditional decorum. I vastly prefer it to an American-style bar, which are often kitschy and loud. It's also the perfect place to eat on your own, since it's relatively casual and the staff are friendly (although, in this instance, amusingly prone to misunderstanding foreign accents).

After dinner, I wandered the downtown causeways of Glasgow, deciding to stop into one more pub to have a beer. The previous night at Oran Mor, I'd tried locally-brewed Tennent lager. Scotland is known more for dark beers, but everywhere has its mass-produced lager. I'd found it rather tasteless the previous night, but I'd already been pretty drunk, so I decided to have another go at it to see if my opinion improved. It didn't, sadly. Tennent is the only real miss in terms of Scottish beverages I tried while in the country, and I decided I'd stick to darker Scottish beers for the remainder of the trip.

Slinking back to the airbnb, I slid into bed and readied for the next day. I loved Glasgow, a fantastic city full of personality, history, and gothic beauty. Tomorrow, I'd begin my journey into a land of castles, legends, and battles of old, at the gateway to the highlands.

Callander

Callander
Gateway to the Highlands

Leaving my airbnb at dawn, I headed to the Glasgow Queen Street Station to catch the next train out of the city. My adventure in Scotland was only just beginning.

I've always had a pleasant experience with Scotrail. It's not quite the Shinkansen or the TGV, but it definitely beats the nightmare on rails that is America's Amtrak. It's efficient, relatively comfortable, and the conductors are always courteous. It's also very cheap, and you can easily and without any confusion buy a ticket from a machine in the station just before your departure.

My destination was the town of Callander, just outside Stirling. That was where Steven was holding his wedding, but it's a scenic, quaint little town that's worth visiting even if you don't have an event drawing you there.

Once seated in the train next to my window seat, it would be a mere 25-minute trip to Stirling. From there, a bus would take me to Callander.

The Victorian streets of Glasgow vanished behind us, and green hills and pastures rolled by. Sheep grazed in fields out my window, occasionally looking up to watch the train thunder past. This was the Scottish countryside as seen in a painting — a land nourished by the ages.

A great hill, atop which sat a walled castle, came into view. Looming over the town below, it sat as a sentry to the lands to the north — Stirling Castle, sight of some of the most famous battles in Scotland's history.

Stirling itself would wait for another day. As I exited the train, I looked up times for the bus to Callander on my phone, only to discover that I had about an hour to kill. Rain began to fall, vista of the town and the castle atop it enveloped in a damp fog — as archetypical an image of Scotland as one could ask for. Without an umbrella (something I would recommend having), I pulled up my jacket's hood and made my way up the street from the station in search of something hot to drink.

"If you don't like the weather in Scotland," Steven had told me a couple days prior, "just wait a few minutes."

This usually holds true, but the sky seemed rather dark and I soon realized that taking a walk into town had not been the wisest course of action. The rain wasn't too bad though, and soon it had slowed to a drizzle in time for me to duck into Bayne's Family Bakers. Getting a cup of relatively decent coffee, I made my way back downhill to the station.

The bus situation in Scotland is confusing, to say the least. Fares change on a whim, pickup locations are not always clear, and stops will sometimes go by local names not listed on Google Maps. I'd apparently be headed to the Callander "war memorial" stop, nearby the AirBNB at which I'd booked my stay for the next two nights.

At the terminal stood a group of older local women.

"Disnae seem to be coming," one said to me.

Indeed, the bus was late.

"Yeah," I laughed. "Wonder what's happening."

"You're from America?" the woman asked in surprise.

"Yeah, my friend is getting married in Callander."

"Well, let's go inside and ask."

HOW TO HAVE AN ADVENTURE IN SCOTLAND

A far cry from the bizarre conversation I'd had in the Glasgow coffee shop, this friendly old lady took me to the counter inside and asked what was happening. As it turned out, the bus number had changed. I'd never have figured it out without her help.

Eventually, the bus arrived to the terminal, and the old ladies (who'd gathered with their friend) and I piled in. The bus driver asked on our way in what our destinations would be. It actually changes what the fare will be, and you pay for your ticket ahead of time.

"The war memorial?" I said, not sure if that was what it was actually called. "Callander."

"The squeer!" one of the old ladies corrected me. "It's in Callander at the squeer."

I thanked the bus driver, and the old lady for giving the correct localized stop name.

Stirling pulled away, and the countryside enveloped us once more. The winding road through the green hills of Scotland's lowlands took us past a few notable places, including Deanston whisky distillery in Doune. I've never had Deanston, which is why it's not in my recommended Scotch list, but I encourage you to try it and let me know how it is. About 45 minutes later, we arrived at the town square.

"Are you meeting your friend at the memorial?" asked the old lady.

"Not yet," I said, "but thanks for your help."

Bidding goodbye to the old ladies and the driver, I stepped out into the light drizzle of rain and found myself in a quaint, idyllic place.

Near the square was a fudge shop, which I made a note to visit. Just behind the fudge shoppe was my accommodation — listed on AirBNB as "The Wee Hoose."

The Wee Hoose was the first accommodation I booked in Scotland, planned around the wedding. I mainly booked it because of the name, but it also had lots of reviews from thrilled customers who'd enjoyed their stay there.

RAFFAEL CORONELLI

A local cat in Callander

HOW TO HAVE AN ADVENTURE IN SCOTLAND

The Wee Hoose

A cat sat behind the fence next to the door to the Hoose. It was the only inhabitant I met on the premises, which leads me believe that the cat was actually the Hoose's owner with whom I'd been communicating. Waving to the bushy little animal, I let myself into the cottage via a lockbox.

A small cottage with stone walls and rustic, classic design, the Wee Hoose was as much of a Scottish Countryside experience as the town in which it resides. It was a little cold on entry, but once I turned on the space heaters in the various rooms, it was extremely cozy.

The Wee Hoose set up for my two-night stay, I ventured around the block to the fudge shoppe. There were a lot of interesting varieties of fudge, made there at the location, but I went for the traditional Scottish Tablet. I'd recommend this, as it's the classic Scottish fudge experience — a big block of fudge-y goodness that crunches and cracks as you eat it. It's not exactly good for your teeth, but you should try it at least once.

RAFFAEL CORONELLI

Callander is called the "Gateway to the Highlands," as it sits on the border between that region and the Lowlands of Scotland's south. One would think that's just a formality, a name to place it on a map — but it really is visually apparent.

Behind the town to the north, looking to the end of the street, loom majestic mid-sized mountain peaks — "munros" — through the mist and overcast clouds. One truly gets the impression that they're right on the verge of Scotland's legendary, wild northern region.

The town itself is essentially one street, but it has everything emblematic of what you'd imagine the Scottish countryside to be. I found it incredibly charming.

In need of facial tissues, I stopped into Tesco. If you're from the US, consider Tesco an equivalent to Walgreens or CVS. It's a convenience store where you can get things you need in a pinch, and you'll probably end up visiting one at least once on your trip. As I am wont to do, I also bought a bottle of rejuvenating Irn Bru and drank it whilst finishing my walk to the edge of town and back.

Callander

I passed a pub with a sign outside advertising "delicious food." It's a pub in the Scottish countryside, so they really don't need to specify what type of delicious food is available. I had all of it several times throughout my trip — haggis (in various forms), bangers & mash, fish & chips, steak pie. I'll give you the rundown as I encountered these, with steak pie and bangers & mash already covered in my Glasgow chapters. For what it's worth, I do consider all of it to count as "delicious food."

I'd be meeting Steven and his wedding party for the pre-wedding dinner, so I headed back to the Wee Hoose to shower and clean up — removing the stench of a travel day from me before putting myself in presentable company.

Unfortunately, the faucet in the shower was strange. By this, I mean that you needed to press a red button on the shower head to get the hot water to turn on. This is apparently common in Britain, but it took me about half an hour to figure it out — and only after messaging the Wee Hoose's owner for instructions.

The intricacies of British plumbing, he joked.

HOW TO HAVE AN ADVENTURE IN SCOTLAND

Steven's parents arrived to pick me up, so I headed out. They took me to an establishment called the Lade Inn — a nice restaurant that offers a fully catered group dinner which the party ordered ahead of time. That was our reason for going there, along with some house-brewed beverages.

The building itself is almost cartoonishly rustic, a quaint little farm-house looking inn that feels like something from another time. The inside is just as atmospheric and homey. It being a wedding party, everyone was seated in a prearranged pattern, and I ended up to just Steven's right with his wife-to-be on his left. Aside from the engaged couple, our Glaswegian griend, and Steven's parents whom I'd briefly met in the car, the rest of the crowd were complete strangers. Luckily, that didn't prove to be a problem.

Everyone was absolutely lovely to talk to, and made me feel welcome with the kind of Scottish hospitality that the lads had shown upon my arrival in Glasgow. I talked to all of them with genuine interest.

The house beer was fantastic. I had the "Ladeout" — dark and rich like the black waters of a Scottish loch. Great stuff if you're as much a fan of dark beers.

My appetizer was Scottish style prawns. Steven's fiancé Laura warned me before its arrival that Scottish prawns are served in a "weird sauce" that I might not be anticipating. It was a sort of milky cream almost like ranch dressing that you wouldn't expect to have with shrimp, but I enjoyed it. Your mileage will vary on that particular dish.

For my entree, there was one thing that I absolutely had to try.

RAFFAEL CORONELLI

A certain menu option piqued my interest above all else — the most legendary food of Scotland, banned in America for it being too wild, too much of the highlands' merciless need to use every last piece of the animal lest the cold munros take back the life they gave.

Two circular blobs of oatmeal and organ meat set down in front of me.

I was about to try haggis.

Haggis is, essentially, a deconstructed sausage with oatmeal in it. Do you know what meat is in a sausage? No? Well, you don't want to find out. Due to unfortunate English propaganda about the "weird uncivilized north," everyone knows that haggis is made out of the "gross stuff."

Think for a moment, though, if any meat is truly without grossness. Just think of a regular sausage made of lamb's meat, and then think of how much more filling it might be mixed with oatmeal — a hardy food for a highlander's dinner.

Taking my first bite, the flavorful, spiced meat and starchy oatmeal blazed across my tastebuds like a blaring bagpipe performance. This wasn't gross — it was delicious! Absolutely bizarre that the only time you hear someone talking about haggis, it's usually in derogatory tones — and then they go and wolf down a McDonald's hamburger. Alas, the power of clown-driven advertising is not behind haggis, but the power of northern tradition certainly is.

This entire page is my defense and genuine praise of one of the world's most unfairly maligned foods. While in Scotland (or in a non-Scottish establishment that miraculously serves it), and you don't have dietary restrictions, you may be tempted to try something new.

Give it a shot, won't you? You might be as surprised as I was to discover my number one favorite food of the Scottish cuisine.

HOW TO HAVE AN ADVENTURE IN SCOTLAND

Haggis at the Lade Inn

As one is wont to do while in Scotland, we moved the party to another pub after dinner. At that point, I was getting to know the crowd, and everyone's excitement for the following day was reaching fever-pitch. Steven and his fiancé were understandably nervous, but it was a nervous excitement more than anything else.

After we'd all had our last glass, we bid farewell for the night and I slagged back down the street to the Wee Hoose — head buzzing with good times — awaiting the following day's extravagant events. I was going to experience a real Scottish wedding.

Loch Venachar
A Real Scottish Party

Cool, early morning air drew me awake as I lay in bed, wrapped up and cozy in the blankets near the space heater in the Wee Hoose's bedroom. Stumbling into the bathroom, the rest of the Hoose was chilly since I'd left the other heaters off during the night. At least I knew how to work the shower, now.

Steaming up the tiny bathroom with my shower, I got ready and put on some clothes — not my full dress clothes for the day's main events, but my usual sweater / dark pants / boots / coat combo to go on a little bit of a stroll on my own to start a magical day in the Scottish countryside.

Breakfast was the first matter to which I needed to attend that morning, and Callander has a fine selection of breakfast options. Fat Jack's is conveniently located right across from the Wee Hoose, but I decided to have that the following morning and instead cross the street and the square to Pip's Coffee and Tea.

Entering Pip's, I found it uninhabited aside from a young woman at the counter who seated me and handed me a menu. I ordered a pot of black breakfast tea and a sausage biscuit. The tea was charmingly served in a full teapot, which you pour for yourself. The sausage was in the traditional square shape that sausages on biscuits take in Scotland. It was the perfect antidote to any chance of a hangover, and the perfect wake-up food.

I sat for a little while, contemplating, draining my teapot and looking out my table side window at the Callander square — or "squeer," as the old lady on the bus had called it. This was a fine morning, and there was a fine day's events to be had ahead of me.

A word of warning that I was not prepared for — Pip's only took cash, so I had to run across the street to the ATM to get some pound banknotes. The waitress was perfectly accommodating and let me do it and come back, which was nice.

My teapot finished and breakfast paid for, I headed west up the street to take a step beyond the town's shops. Turning left, I found myself looking at an idyllic landscape — a sunny glen, green and dewy in the chilly morning.

Pip's Coffee and Tea

HOW TO HAVE AN ADVENTURE IN SCOTLAND

A river — the River Teith — babbled as it had in ages past. Before it, in the middle of the glen, arose a green mound with wooden steps leading to its summit.

Tom Na Chisaig is a mysterious mound of earth, possibly a motte or former sight of a castle, dating to around the 12th century. Little is known about its exact origins, who built it, and why. It's been there since the Middle Ages, watching over the town of Callander and the river that flows by it from a height of around five meters.

Tom Na Chisaig

RAFFAEL CORONELLI

Callander from the top of Tom Na Chisaig

Morning dew and soft earth squished around my boots as I stepped up to Tom Na Chisaig and began climbing the heavily weathered steps to its short summit. That same ground had been walked in centuries past by whomever to which the land had belonged, whomever had built the motte — people whose creation remained, weathered but strong, at the foot of the highlands.

Reaching the top, I stood and looked out at the town — the ever flowing river — the towering munro peaks in the distance. It was quiet. I was alone with the ghosts of kings, wind blowing gently across the glen.

The moment passed, as it had for all those who'd stood at that spot in times now long gone. I stepped down from Tom Na Chisaig and wandered further along the path by the river.

A man walked his dog by the riverbank. Two children played in the grass under a tree. The river flowed on toward Loch Venachar. I, too, would be making my way there later in the day. I passed a stone wall covered in moss and ivy. Reaching out and running my hand across it as I passed, I breathed in the dewy air, sun bathing my face.

On the steps of Tom Na Chisaig

RAFFAEL CORONELLI

I returned to the Hoose to change clothes for an event for the ages — a Scottish wedding at the shore of Loch Venachar. Steven instructed me to head to their hotel around midday, so I had a little bit of time to get myself presentable.

After freshening up and dressing myself in a subtle dark blue tartan-patterned dress jacket and reasonably dressy pants, I walked up the street to the hotel Steven and his wedding entourage were staying. Upon arriving in Steven's room, I was greeted by him and his groomsmen dressed in a manner that I have to describe as "awesome."

Dress jacket tops and tuxedos, of course, were worn by all — along with bright tartan kilts with ornate pouches and other features hanging off of them. Suddenly, even though my jacket was alright, my pants felt woefully inadequate. Where was my kilt? Was I a coward and a fool for not wearing one? I guess, as a foreigner, I was given a pass. At least I didn't have the pressure of being a groomsman myself, so I wouldn't be throwing off the pre-planned uniform. Steven was all nerves, as is to be expected of someone about to be married, but was welcoming and in good spirits.

After chatting for a little while, it was time for the wedding party (plus me, who didn't otherwise have a vehicle) to pile into a small rented bus and head to the venue — Venachar Lochside. As the name suggests, it's a rentable wedding and event venue complete with a bar that resides at the shore of the magnificent Loch Venachar. The bus rolled out of the town of Callander, by pastures where sheep grazed. Then the loch came into view — surrounded by munros, sun glinting off its surface.

HOW TO HAVE AN ADVENTURE IN SCOTLAND

Loch Venachar

Scotland's lochs are not just lakes, but have a specific definition similar in origin to Norwegian fjords — bodies of water that were gouged into mountain ranges as glacial drift and ice ages tore into Northern Europe. The British Isles are geologically part of the European continent, rather than separately formed volcanic islands. Lochs stand as a remnant of the Earth's power to rip continents asunder and cut through them with great sheets of ice kilometers thick.

The ceremony was held outside on a deck area right on Loch Venachar. It was suitably emotional, the unbelievable vista that served as its backdrop amplifying everything about it. Cold wind blasted me in my lochside seat, but it was all part of the deal. I actually received an indirect shoutout during the ceremony itself, with the woman officiating announcing that people had come from "as far away as Chicago."

Then, inside, the reception party began. There were about sixty or so people in attendance, all Scottish except for myself, our Glaswegian friend's American emigrant wife, the French wife of one of their friends, and Steven's sister's Englishman partner Chris. There was beer out, so I grabbed one before we'd begin drinking from the bar.

As I chatted with Steven's father, his attention turned to the loch outside.

"You've heard of Nessie," he said.

"Yeah, of course," I laughed.

"Have you heard of Vinnie?"

This was a revelation that piqued my interest.

"Vinnie?" I asked, wondering where this was going.

He proceeded to explain to me that a loch monster, Vinnie, lives in Loch Venachar. I'm not sure what spurred the narrative, but we'd had a few drinks and he was having fun. The more I listened to him talk about Vinnie, the more I realized that this creature deserves to be canonized as one of the great creatures of Scotland's modern mythology. Hopefully this book will bring monster enthusiasts to Callander in search of Vinnie, who I assure you is definitely real and not something that Steven's dad invented as a joke.

Vinnie — artist's rendition by Alex Gayhart

Vinnie the Loch Venachar Monster
drawn by Alex Gayhart

RAFFAEL CORONELLI

The author of this book (left) with just-married Steven (right)

Steven's sister Alannah took it upon herself to give me a rundown of scotches to drink whilst in Scotland. This turned out to be incredibly helpful, and gave me a roadmap for my beverage consumption on the rest of the trip. She began my indoctrination by getting me a Laphroaig from the bar — a delicious, peat-heavy taste that I consider ideal for Scotch.

Whisky in hand, it was time to head up to dinner. I was seated at the "Godzilla" table. Steven and I met at a Godzilla convention years back, and here I was at his wedding in Scotland. Life is a series of totally inexplicable events, when it comes down to it.

HOW TO HAVE AN ADVENTURE IN SCOTLAND

Dinner was a Scottish hen, which was delicious — not quite as adventurous as the previous night's haggis extravaganza, but there was nothing to complain about. Also, there was wine on the table. I was already drinking an incredible Scotch, but free wine is free wine. I'm not sure if it was the wisest decision, but I was having a good time and I figured it was time to begin double-fisting.

At this point, the events of the evening become less clear.

While the party moved down to the dance floor, I remember chatting with other guests and discussing my trip. Chris was very intent on giving me advice, since he'd lived in Inverness for a little while.

"Inverness?" he said skeptically. "What'll you do there?"

"Well, a day trip to Loch Ness," I said. "Then another day to see the city itself."

"You'll be kicking your feet in Inverness," he shook his head. "You'll be bored! Go to the Isle of Skye for the day instead. It's the best Scotland has to offer."

I wasn't sure I'd be bored in Inverness, but the Isle of Skye was an intriguing suggestion. Getting to the out-of-the-way isle would involve booking a guide to take me there and back in a day. I could handle that. There was something about it that felt more adventurous than poking around another mid-sized Scottish city — and in truth, I hadn't heard of a lot about things to actually do in Inverness proper. I'd keep his suggestion in mind.

Another guy told me a joke about someone selling "eight leg of venison," but I was so drunk and his Scots dialect so thick that I legitimately thought he was talking about an "eight-legged venison." Add a spider-deer to the list of amazing creatures for which you should be on the lookout when you come to Scotland, alongside Nessie and Loch Venachar's own Vinnie.

Music played by the wedding DJ that night of course included The Proclaimers' Scottish anthem "I'm Gonna Be (500 Miles)" to which everyone sang along. A fitting song for an international voyage.

The evening's final song, which involved another singalong from everyone in attendance, was Scottish rock band Runrig's rendition of the traditional song "Loch Lomond". Apparently, "Loch Lomond" is the song that closes out every single Scottish event — whether it's a wedding, a regular party, or a night at a nightclub.

"You'll take the high road
And I'll take the low road
And I'll be in Scotland before you,
Where me and my true love
Will never meet again
On the bonny bonny banks of Loch Lomond."

I would indeed be taking a different road and going a different way than the others. I'd made friends at the wedding, and took part in something special with the ones I already had. I got to experience a total immersion in Scottish culture that you wouldn't get at a celebration elsewhere.

Apparently, the wedding party drank the bar dry.

Steven and Laura would soon be off on their honeymoon to Tokyo. I told him I'd follow along online. I'd been in the midst of planning a trip to Japan for myself at the end of the year, one somewhat in the style of my adventure through Scotland. We said we'd meet again, bidding farewell with a "see you next time."

I'd been welcomed into a fully Scottish event in a way that many who visit don't get to experience. Having close friends there helps. It was a night to remember on the bonny, bonny banks of Loch Venachar.

Venachar Lochside

Stirling

Stirling
Battleground of the Ages

At some point in the previous evening, a screw on my glasses had gotten loose, causing the left lens to pop out of its frame. I was having to hold it in place, but I decided I'd have to deal with it if I had time before the bus to Stirling arrived at the town square.

First, I had to eat. I'd done a light breakfast of the sausage biscuit and tea the previous morning, and I was a bit hungover from the night's reveling. I needed something hardier, something that would fill me with a smorgasbord of bloody northern delicacies. I needed a traditional, Full Scottish Breakfast.

For that, I'd be traveling mere meters from the door of the Wee Hoose to Fat Jack's restaurant. The cool countryside air, wet with a light drizzle of rain, greeted me as I stepped outside. It was another picturesque morning in Callander — but my stomach was telling me with urgency that I needed sustenance, so I hurried inside.

Seated with my coffee slowly drawing me into consciousness, I awaited my food. Aerosmith's "I Don't Want to Miss a Thing" played over the speakers — which was pretty weird for the atmosphere, but the restaurant seemed to be manned by an early morning staff of young people about my own age. I'd worked in food service before and sometimes whatever comes up on the randomized playlist is what comes up, and there's nothing anyone can do about it.

Other than the music, the place itself was charming and rustic, with dark wooden tables and walls.

Then, my food arrived. A full Scottish breakfast consists of an assortment of the following items: toast, roasted tomatoes, sliced mushrooms, sausage links, bacon, and black and/or white pudding.

White pudding is similar to haggis, combining organ meat (usually pork) with oatmeal or barley. Black pudding, which I was served at Fat Jack's, is identical in concept to its white counterpart except that it contains blood. Yes, blood! Like Dracula! It's delicious, actually, and one of my favorite Scottish foods. When given the option for a full Scottish breakfast further along on my trip, the savory and vampiric dish was always what I looked forward to the most. Even if you're put off by the concept, barring dietary restrictions, I really think you should give black pudding a chance. It's a case of consuming another part of the animal that you already would've been eating anyway — barring dietary restrictions.

Full of blood and other delicious foods, I strode like a resurrected Transylvanian count out of Fat Jack's as The Backstreet Boys' "Everybody (Backstreet's Back)" played over the speakers. There was one thing left to do — resurrect my glasses, of which I now had to hold the left lens in place with my hand to keep it from falling out onto the street.

Luckily, it didn't take me long to find a great hardware store colorfully named "Screw It", run by an old local man. I found exactly what I needed — a kit of tiny jewelry screwdrivers, perfect to tighten the screw on my glasses. Sure enough, it worked perfectly, and I didn't have to worry about losing my means of vision for the rest of the trip.

With that, I packed up my things and said goodbye to the Wee Hoose. I couldn't have asked for more of a charming place to stay. Shutting the door, I passed the fudge shop one last time to catch the bus at the square where it'd dropped me off.

HOW TO HAVE AN ADVENTURE IN SCOTLAND

Full Scottish Breakfast and Fat Jack's in Callander

RAFFAEL CORONELLI

Boarding the bus, I was surprised to learn that the fare back to Stirling was nearly double what it had been on the way there. This is normal for Scotland, as apparently bus fares fluctuate seemingly at random. I asked my Scottish friends about it later, and they said they had no idea why it happens. Get ready for a surprise when you get your money out for the bus ticket.

"Your ticket!" the bus driver called after me as I took my seat. "Sir, your ticket!"

Oh, yeah. You need your ticket to get off the bus, so make sure you take it.

My destination would be another two-night stay, a place I'd only briefly seen from the train station. I was headed to a medieval city that was the sight of historic battles, and one of the most important and impressive castles in Scotland — Stirling.

Along the way, we picked up a few more passengers headed in my direction. A young man boarded and told the driver that he was going to Doune. The driver told him the fare, and he had to do a double-take. This was an especially expensive day for the bus route — just my luck. Oh, well, it was on my schedule and it was worth it for the transport.

The bus left me at much the same place it had picked me up outside the station. From there, I made my way uphill and into town. Much of Stirling is sandwiched between two prominent landmarks — the magnificent castle, and the obelisk-like hilltop tower that comprises the William Wallace Monument (more on him in a bit). My accommodation was a traditional Bed and Breakfast called the Old Tram House, closer to the Wallace Monument, which meant I had a bit of a trek across town ahead of me.

Stirling's medieval streets wind and twist up and down the hillsides, close-knit buildings comprising a tight and economical townscape in the castle's shadow. Through the center of town runs the River Forth — and across it, Stirling Old Bridge.

HOW TO HAVE AN ADVENTURE IN SCOTLAND

Stirling Old Bridge

This bridge was built around the year 1500, but on its site was an even older stone bridge. It was there in 1297 that William Wallace lead the Scots in the Battle of Stirling Bridge.

The free Scottish army had established a camp on Abbey Craig, the current site of the Wallace Monument. They knew that if they could drive away the English forces from Stirling, they'd win Scotland outright due to its strategic position. The English army, a force of trained infantry lead by battle-hardened knights equipped with the latest in armor and weaponry, amassed on the opposite side of the River Forth — ready to quell what was seen as little more than a troublesome uprising. Wallace knew that the river was key to the Scots' advantage — all they had to do was wait on the opposite side of Stirling Bridge.

Castle Hill across the Stirling Old Bridge

The bridge framed Wallace's vision, short stone walls giving him focus on the enemy soldiers on the other side. There was no other way to cross. They would come to him.

At last, a shout sounded from the English ranks. The order had been given. Knights, fully clad in their head-to-toe armor and wielding great broadswords that could cut a man in half, stepped onto the bridge. The sound of metal hitting stone echoed to the ears of the Scots — the sound of advancing doom. Still, Wallace held fast and did not give the order to attack.

Infantry amassed alongside the knights, though they had to travel in shorter ranks in order to cross the narrow bridge. This was all part of Wallace's plan. Soon, the English had marched nearly half-way.

Heart pounding, he watched the knights get closer. Inhuman helmets hid their faces, but he could nearly see their eyes through the visors. They were confident — if only because they'd underestimated their disadvantage until it was too late.

HOW TO HAVE AN ADVENTURE IN SCOTLAND

Seeing that the English had advanced far enough, Wallace gave the order. He and his warriors stormed onto the bridge — blades swinging — and met the opposition head-on.

The English knights' massive swords cut through the bodies of the first of the Scotsmen like butter knives through black pudding. Then, the confines of their environment came into play. Designed for an open battlefield, the knights' heavy armor proved less effective against the concentrated wall of death raging from the end of the bridge.

Steel scraped and bone shattered. Dismembered limbs dropped to the ground beneath the clashing armies pushing against each other in the tight space of the bridge. Blood painted the stones and cascaded over the sides. The River Forth ran a deep shade of red.

By the end of that violent day, the Scots had driven back their opposition. Stirling was undisputedly in Scottish control.

It was a historic defeat of the English and one of the decisive moments in the First War of Scottish Independence. I embellished some minor details in my retelling just now, but I did make sure the geography and historical accuracy was there. A wildly inaccurate version of this battle was portrayed on screen in the movie *Braveheart*, which for some reason neglected the bridge entirely.

Despite the battle not being captured in exactly the correct light and its main landmark missing from the film, *Braveheart* may be the reason most foreigners will know of Stirling and have a connection to the historical events that took place there. William Wallace was indeed a big deal in Scottish history, and his connection to Stirling is the reason the great monument to his memory towers over the north end of the city.

As I walked across Stirling Bridge, I could almost hear the swords clashing on shields, the yells of warriors in centuries past holding the strategic crossing of the River Forth at that exact spot. The bridge was different, and all those men were long since dead, but that same crossing at that same strategic point was getting me to where I needed to go. William Wallace held the Stirling Bridge in 1297 for freedom of the Scots, and I crossed it get to my Bed and Breakfast in 2019. They can take our lives, but they can't take our breakfast!

Speaking of having one's life taken, I learned a terrifying fact about Scotland as I stepped off the bridge and across the following intersection to continue my walk up Causewayhead Road to the Old Tram House. In the middle of the street, I heard the roaring motor of a bus grow closer, prompting me to sprint out of the way before the vehicle barreled past me — nearly mowing me down. It didn't even slow, or acknowledge that it had rounded a corner and nearly flattened me.

This is because, in the UK, pedestrians do not always have the right of way. This comes as a shock to someone from the US, where it's the driver's fault if a pedestrian is hit under any circumstances. I'm not particularly litigious, but I do find that the rule makes drivers marginally more careful not to hit pedestrians. In the United Kingdom, you can be turned into pudding in the road and it's all your fault! Please don't let that happen to you, especially since it takes some getting used to the vehicles coming from the opposite direction.

The rest of my walk down Causewayhead Road wasn't nearly as eventful or dangerous. One after another, I passed traditional inns. I guess that stretch of road could be considered a "Bed and Breakfast district" because you're really spoiled for choice. Eventually I reached the one at which I'd booked my two-night stay, the Old Tram House.

HOW TO HAVE AN ADVENTURE IN SCOTLAND

William Wallace Monument, visible from the Old Tram House

Charming, ivy-accented exterior gave way to an entry hall that instantly transported me into a countryside-set BBC programme (my frame of reference for this type of environment). My boots creaked the wood floorboards underneath, acoustics causing the sound to become even more prominent as it echoed through the quiet room containing a staircase, a small desk, and doors leading elsewhere in the house. This was already a bigger and more inn-like establishment than the Wee Hoose.

An older man greeted me, and I apologized for arriving too early for check-in. He said it was fine, and offered me tea and biscuits, as it was the early afternoon. The level of hospitality practically floored me, and the tea and biscuits were delicious. I sat to eat them in a fully furnished waiting room that felt more like a room in a manor house — covered in ornate wallpaper, art fixtures, and statuary.

There was still a bit of time before I could officially check in (the woman who ran that part of the operation was out until then) so I asked if I could leave my luggage there and go on a walk. He happily obliged, and I headed up the road to Abbey Craig — the towering hill on which sits the William Wallace Memorial.

"Make sure you see the Mad Max statue in Stirling," my dad had told me before my trip.

It had taken me a second to register what he was talking about. There was, in years past, a statue of Mel Gibson as *Braveheart*'s version of William Wallace at the memorial. Probably due to its historical inaccuracy and somewhat comical presence, the statue is no longer there. In fact, the entire memorial was undergoing a thorough renovation at the time of my visit, but I still wanted to go up to the peak of Abbey Craig and see it. It's impressive enough, even without a statue resembling the titular character of *Mad Max Beyond Thunderdome*.

The base of Abbey Craig is a nondescript gate to a public park leading off from a roundabout. Step through it, and you're on a path winding through a field, around a bend, and up into a steeply inclining forest. Back and forth the trail winds, past interesting carved wooden figures showing elements of Scotland's history. These are great, rustic pieces that fit naturally with the environment around them.

As I neared the summit, the steep incline really started to get to me. The climb is hard, even if you're in relatively good shape. The real killer, though, was the wind. Blaring through the trees, the atmospheric waves threatened to rip me off the side of the mountain like an angry god who didn't want me ascending to the top.

Stirling from the side of Abbey Craig

Then, around the last bend — out of breath, and almost hurdling over the cliff face — I saw the base of the monument. Piercing skyward, the obelisk-like castle tower symbolizes the triumph of Wallace and all he did for Scotland. Its majesty is amplified by the place it sits. From its base, you can see Stirling below, the bridge where the battle took place, and the hilltop castle beyond.

I'm not exaggerating when I say that I had to literally hold onto a fence to stop from flying off the mountaintop. I'm not sure how normal that level of wind is, but it was absolutely terrifying — a violent simulation of being locked in battle with the English army. I survived, but it felt thrilling in a way that honored the monument's subject matter.

Arriving back at the Old Tram House, I was able to check in. My room was a suite on the top floor, which I'd gotten for a deal that almost felt criminal on my part considering how nice it was. Truly, I felt like a king. Looking out my window, I saw the Wallace Monument atop the hill to which I'd just climbed. This was the perfect place to end my first day in Stirling.

As I fell into bed, completely exhausted, I thought about the time ahead of me. I still had the castle and the rest of Stirling to explore — then, on to the highlands.

"You'll be kicking your feet in Inverness," Chris' warning rang out in my mind as the sun set over Stirling. *"You'll be bored!"*

Opening my phone, I entered "Isle of Skye tours from Inverness" into the search engine.

Left: View from the top suite in the Old Tram House

William Wallace Monument

The Palace at Stirling Castle

Stirling Castle
Throne of Scotland

The top floor suite of the Old Tram House felt more luxurious than the price would indicate. I slept like a log in my royal accommodations, waking up to the sun streaming in through the curtains from past the Wallace Monument out the window. I was awakening like a king, sprawled out on the bed in the finest room of the inn, ready to make a full day of kingly spectacle and history. Indeed, today was a day to explore a castle.

After cleaning myself up and stumbling downstairs, I entered the breakfast room — set up with fine china dishes and enough space for a banquet. There was only myself and two others, an elderly couple who introduced themselves as former locals who now resided in Nova Scotia. They were lovely people, and we chatted about what we'd be doing that day.

"Seems like it might rain," the man said.

"Well my Scottish friend told me that if you don't like the weather in Scotland, just wait five minutes," I grinned, relaying Steven's joke.

"What cheek," he laughed.

I'd had an excellent bed, so now it was time for the other end of the deal — breakfast. I'd of course requested the full Scottish breakfast, and it did not disappoint in the slightest. Black pudding, sausage, bacon, tomatoes, mushrooms — everything needed to begin a day spent visiting a place that had once been the site of unimaginable bloodshed and the horrors of medieval war.

Full of my full Scottish breakfast, I headed down Causewayhead Road to the bridge. Advancing toward the hilltop castle, I noted how attacking armies must have felt trying to cross the river to the fortress on the other side — an ominous sight to encroach upon.

The bridge was inhabited by a few other pedestrians that morning, either going into the city for their daily activities or just going for a stroll. Walking in front of me was a young man in a punk-rock-styled outfit, including a leather jacket across the back of which he'd painted a very clear and unambiguous message:

"F**K THE TORIES."

I laughed to myself. The spirit of William Wallace was alive and well on Stirling Bridge.

From the bridge, it's actually a little bit of a complicated route up to the castle. Follow Crofthead Road up to Lower Castlehill and take a right to begin your final ascent. If you get lost, don't fret — I did as well, and had to consult Google Maps on how to get there. Meandering through the hillside streets, I stopped and absentmindedly leaned against a building to get my bearings via my phone.

"HULLOOOOOO!" a deep, jovial, slightly annoyed voice sounded from inside.

I hadn't realized that I'd leaned against the side of someone's house right next to their window. Don't do this. Embarrassed, I laughed and continued uphill.

Full Scottish Breakfast at the Old Tram House

RAFFAEL CORONELLI

Castle Hill

The incline is steep. Like the other pinnacle, the Wallace Monument, you'll be out of breath by the time you reach the ramparts. This is a key strategic point for the fortress — attackers had to climb and expend their energy fighting a literal uphill battle whilst being bombarded from the ramparts above. As a result, Stirling Castle is almost impossible to take and a traditional ground attack is inadvisable, in case you're planning on invading for some reason (please don't do that).

This was the exact position in which the English found themselves in 1304. William Wallace had finally been defeated, but Scottish forces under the command of William Oliphant held Stirling — the strategic point the English needed to regain control of Scotland.

The ensuing siege lasted months. The English deployed every known tactic, but their invading forces could not scale the hill and reach the castle without suffering terrible losses.

HOW TO HAVE AN ADVENTURE IN SCOTLAND

That was until King Edward the First decided to make a last-ditch effort for victory and ordered the construction of a medieval super-weapon the likes of which had never been seen.

Towering over the treetops at the base of the hill, a wooden structure rose up to face down the castle walls. It was the Warwolf, the largest trebuchet ever built, meant to annihilate a hilltop castle wall with one blow.

Records of the Warwolf's exact size are dodgy at best. Some outlandish internet claims that I haven't been able to properly source say that it was more than a hundred meters in height (between three and four hundred feet). This sounds a little ridiculous, considering the physics of building a mechanical device like that out of wood, so let's say that it was realistically closer to one hundred feet (about thirty meters). That would still make it incomparably large for a siege weapon, more than three times the size of a standard trebuchet.

At beginning of the fourteenth century, the circumstances of its launch must have been akin to the detonation of a nuclear warhead. English soldiers ducked and covered their ears as the gears spun. The gargantuan counterweight, weighing tons, dropped forward. A boulder hurdled through the air at terrifying speeds that knocked the wind out of the way before it — impacting the wall with a cacophonous explosion of noise and obliterating it like a fist punching through a sheet of paper.

Inside, the projectile splattered men into mulch and stone into dust as it pulverized its way through the Scottish ranks. Survivors with enough time to process what had happened had never experienced anything like it — carnage and pieces of the impenetrable castle wall scattered about the newly made ruin. Only after this annihilating device was deployed did the Scots surrender, finally turning Stirling over to British rule.

Stirling Castle Esplanade

Launching myself over the top of the hill like a rock thrown from the Warwolf, I gazed upon the walls of the castle in admiration. While the architecture of the castle beyond the walls is varied and interesting, the outside is a formidable slab that promises not to let though any enemy who's managed to make it that far.

A statue of legendary Scottish hero Robert the Bruce, erected in modern times, stands watch outside the entrance to the castle. It was next to this statue that I asked a man who seemed to be from Spain to take my picture with the castle walls in the background.

The author of this book at Stirling Castle

Statue of Robert the Bruce at Stirling Castle

Stirling Castle Forework from the Queen Anne Gardens

In the queue to get in, I surveyed the options for entry fee and noticed a fantastic deal. For about sixty pounds, you could get a seven-day pass to any publicly owned castle in Scotland. I knew I'd be visiting at least two others, including Edinburgh and Urquhart, so I naturally went with that option.

I also recommend getting the audio guide. It comes with the pass, and the wealth of information contained in it as you traverse the castle is more than I could ever possibly convey in this book — hours of curated museum-level presentations compiled by scholars and experts to give you all the histories of all the details of the castle. The knowledge you'll gain from it is invaluable. It's where I got a crash course on Stirling history, some of its knowledge I've now been able to relay to you.

Passage between the Palace and Great Hall

A cannon station with the Wallace Monument visible across the town

Aside from the actual history of the place, it really did feel staggering to wander through the courtyards around the centuries-old fortress. So much had happened here in this place — the battlements with their cannons at the ready, the portcullises waiting to slam shut and stop adversaries from advancing further.

I gazed out at Stirling from a cannon station. The small bridge was far below, the monument sticking up beyond it.

HOW TO HAVE AN ADVENTURE IN SCOTLAND

I climbed into a rifleman's port and peered out through the small hole from which he could've surveyed the countryside beneath.

It was from a post like that one that a British rifleman would've fought the oncoming army of the Jacobite rebellion in 1746. The Jacobites were an attempt to regain Scottish independence once again, though they were less successful than Wallace and his legendary ilk, as they were less equipped and had to take on the forces of an ever-strengthening British Empire. They lacked the resources to build a super-weapon like the Warwolf, and as such, were unable to take the otherwise impenetrable fortress from the British.

Looking down from the rifle port, I pictured what it was like to aim and pick off ascending troops coming up the hill. That's the advantage of the castle made clear — the high ground and its solid construction combined to make it the best of its kind at its purpose.

RAFFAEL CORONELLI

The insides of the castle were just as impressive — massive chambers and winding corridors. On the side of one of the older wings of the castle stand monstrous gargoyles depicting demonic figures meant to ward off intruders with visages of the devil.

A demonic gargoyle outside the Palace building

Interior of the Great Hall

RAFFAEL CORONELLI

The Palace

On a purely personal level, Stirling Castle had a certain significance as a place I'd set one of my fictional stories, the climax of my novel <u>Mokwa: Lifesblood of the Earth</u> — wherein a giant frog monster perches atop the castle and plunges the surrounding area into a reign of terror. I hadn't visited the castle before writing it, but somehow that connection felt more justified afterward.

Since the visit, I've included it in two more of my novels to varying degrees. Including the book you're currently reading, Stirling Castle appears in four books I've written to this point, which might make me appear somewhat obsessed with the location.

HOW TO HAVE AN ADVENTURE IN SCOTLAND

The Castle and Stirling below

More than that, the castle's history and grandeur left a terrific impression. Out of all the castles I visited on my trip, Stirling gets my highest recommendation and should be on anyone's list of destinations in Scotland.

A quick visit to the gift shop lead to me buying a Christmas tree ornament in the shape of the castle. There are lots of interesting souvenirs, so it's worth a look around.

The Castle Ramparts

Fish and chips at the Portcullis

HOW TO HAVE AN ADVENTURE IN SCOTLAND

The castle's exploration finished and an appetite worked up, it was time for lunch. My favorite place I ate in Stirling shares the castle mount, a rustic pub called The Portcullis. The menu was the perfect selection of Scottish pub food, the service was friendly, and it's a great place to sit and unwind after exploring.

I ordered fish and chips, and I don't know if it was the atmosphere combined with my appetite, but it was some of the best I've ever had. To drink, I ordered a Belhaven. This might be my favorite Scottish beer — a dark ale with a strong, rich taste.

The Portcullis' atmosphere, quality of the food, and proximity to the castle make it a must-visit if you plan on eating and grabbing a drink while in Stirling.

I spent the rest of the day wandering through the streets of Stirling. At one point, a car drove past and I heard someone scream my name. It was such an abrupt moment that at first I thought someone was targeting me in a drive-by attack. It turned out that it was Steven — who hadn't yet left for Japan. I had to text him my response, as I'd ducked in terror when it happened.

I had a low-key evening for my last in Stirling, resting up in my kingly accommodations at the Old Tram House. The next day, I'd be back on the train, going north — to a land more mysterious, more untamed, full of murkier legends and realms of fantasy. At last, I'd be venturing into the highlands.

Glenmoriston
Outside Inverness

Inverness
The Highlands

"This place has been fantastic," I said to one of the owners of the Old Tram House as I checked out. "It's what I'd hoped staying in Scotland would be like."

I wasn't lying. The place was beautifully decorated, comfortable, and the food was fantastic. The Old Tram House was my favorite hotel at which I stayed on my trip to Scotland, and I'd recommend it to anyone.

After my final delicious, full Scottish breakfast in the fancy dining room, it was off to the station. One last time, I walked Stirling Bridge — meandered through the snaking hillside streets — looked up to the hilltop castle, watching over the town.

There was one nearby attraction that I'd be remiss not to mention, even though I'm remiss to not have actually seen it — the Kelpies. These massive metal statues of horse heads, erected in recent years as a boon for tourists, are in Falkirk, which is about halfway between Stirling and Edinburgh. I just didn't have time for them, but they look very impressive, and tie to the Scottish Kelpie legend of a shape-shifting horse mermaid who comes out of the water to drag unsuspecting seaside people to their watery demise. It's a great legend and an impressive sculpture, so go a bit south if you have time.

I'd be taking two trains that day — first from Stirling to Perth, then switching to a northward line up to Inverness. The ride to Perth was a short one. I'd like to have seen more of the city, but I really only saw the station.

Perth's train station is a bit different than Stirling's. For one, it's bigger and has more tracks. This meant that I had to find my way around the various platforms. It makes sense, as Perth is a fair bit bigger than Stirling as a city. Maybe next time I visit Scotland I'll make it a stop — or maybe you should spend an afternoon there on your way north. Or, go a little bit east to Dundee, a charming-looking coastal city with a river and a cool statue of a dragon. Go on, don't just do everything exactly as I did! Make your own decisions and choose your own adventure!

The train left Perth Station, due north. Scenery became bumpier, rolling meadows becoming foothills of something larger that I'd only glimpsed from the edges of Callander.

Right:
Perth Station

92

HOW TO HAVE AN ADVENTURE IN SCOTLAND

My wonderment was interrupted, rather rudely, by the realization that my phone was nearly out of battery. My solution to this is not something that you should try to replicate. Do not make demands that people treat you with upmost generosity. All this shows is that if you behave respectfully and encounter someone nice, you'll be rewarded.

"Excuse me," I got the conductor's attention. "Is there a charge port near here?"

Often, ScotRail trains will have power outlets — or "charge ports" as they're called in the UK — by every seat. Predominantly, these trains are assigned to busy routes, like going between Glasgow and Edinburgh. Inverness is a bit more out of the way, so this train wasn't quite as luxuriously equipped.

"Hmm," he looked around. "There are some in First Class."

"Oh," I said, disappointed at the idea that I'd have to sit in the station at Inverness and charge my phone in order to find the hotel. "Thanks anyway."

"Well," he continued, looking around again as if to see if anyone was listening in. "If it's important that you charge your phone... Just go on up there. It's fine, there are empty seats."

Profusely thanking the conductor, I got up and moved forward in the train. Just like that, my seat had been upgraded. The sliding door to the first class opened to a quiet interior. Only about three other seats were occupied. How nice, I thought, that the conductor decided to give space in an undersold First Class cabin to someone who genuinely needed it. What a wonderful man, and what a wonderful society we'd have if more people did the same.

Plugging in my phone on the seat side table, I turned my attention out the window — and my breath left me.

RAFFAEL CORONELLI

Cairngorms

Mountains, great snowy peaks thundered past. The train had entered Cairngorms National Park. Cutting latitudinally through the center of the highlands, Cairngorms is a magnificent stretch of the mountain range of the same name that stands between the lowland cities and Inverness. It's the largest national park in the UK, let alone Scotland.

Alongside a glistening mountain river, the train enveloped in the otherwise untouched natural landscape, I could feel that we were in a different part of Scotland. We'd crossed through the Pass of Drumochter and were barreling into an antediluvian land unchanged since time immemorial.

There's something Scandinavian about the landscape of the Scottish highlands, more so than it resembles England to the south. Rocky crags protrude skyward, winding rivers lined with frost flow from the peaks, an overcast sky bares down a wall of mist from the atmosphere to the ground. It feels like another world, filled with mystery.

HOW TO HAVE AN ADVENTURE IN SCOTLAND

The River Garry in Cairngorms National Park

RAFFAEL CORONELLI

It was about three hours before we pulled in to Inverness. The low-lying skyline looked a bit less prominent than Glasgow, or as medieval in layout as Stirling. It was boxier, more utilitarian. This was a city of twentieth-century industry, overhung by a grey sky. As I wandered from the station toward my hotel, the streets appeared a bit grungier — not that I'm criticizing that aesthetic, as I found it to have its own certain charm.

I stopped into an oversized Tesco to buy some necessities I'd neglected to bring with on the trip. Inside, they were playing a song by English rapper Example from about a decade before. Naturally, I bought an Irn Bru.

I later discussed Inverness' vibe with my Scottish friends, and they all had the same view. This was a working class city that had been left behind by the UK's lopsided 1980's economy and never quite returned. Tourism is a big industry now, but much of the city feels a decade in the past — like it's still running to catch up.

On a different note — at least until the time of Brexit, Inverness has been a destination for Polish immigrants to the UK. I heard Polish spoken aloud several times on the street, which was interesting in the context of a highland Scottish city. It makes sense, and it provides Inverness with its own unique immigrant culture.

The Polish connection in Inverness actually dates back nearly half a millennium. Trading routes through Scandinavia via the North Sea brought Polish traders embarking from Gdańsk to Scottish ports. This developed a cultural relationship and exchange between Poland and the Scottish highlands throughout the times Scotland was actively fighting with English armies advancing from the south. I learned all this from my tour guide at Loch Ness, an incredibly knowledgeable guy.

One part of the city that does not underwhelm in the slightest is the part where you'll do most of your sightseeing — the riverfront.

HOW TO HAVE AN ADVENTURE IN SCOTLAND

The River Ness

    The River Ness flows south through the center of the city, emptying into the eponymous loch a bit of a ways past the outskirts. Bridges cross the river at regular intervals, some for pedestrians only. It's a great way to stop and admire the Victorian style architecture of the riverfront — and above it all on a hill, Inverness Castle.

    The castle isn't Stirling — it's rather small, built in the nineteenth century on the site of an older fortress that wasn't siege-resistant enough to make it out of the Middle Ages without being totally obliterated. Still, the current hilltop structure is worth a look. To further entice, it's adjacent to an excellent pub called the Castle Tavern.

Inverness Castle

Highland beef stew at Hootananny

HOW TO HAVE AN ADVENTURE IN SCOTLAND

Also in the vicinity of the castle was my accommodation for the next three nights — the Redcliffe Hotel. Situated in an old fashioned building, the Redcliffe has a number of varying options ranging from renting an entire guest house on the premises to the far cheaper room that I went with. Mine was a compact single bedroom for one person. The size of the room felt more akin to a Japanese business hotel than something one would find in Scotland, but that was just fine for me. It was highly affordable, too, and its convenient proximity to the castle and riverfront made it an excellent place to stay. Inverness was, after all, a base of operations for the next two days' trips elsewhere.

For dinner, I went to a place called Hootananny. Hootananny apparently has live Celtic music later in the evening, but I was there early since I was hungry after the day of traveling. I had an excellent beef stew, the service was very friendly, and the and decor was as one would expect from a good, traditional Scottish establishment. I only ate at two restaurants in Inverness, one of them twice, but Hootananny gets a thumbs up from me for their delicious Scottish cuisine and lively atmosphere.

Post-Hootananny, I wandered around the riverfront for the remainder of the evening — stopping on one of the bridges to admire the River Ness as it flowed beneath my feet. The dark waters cutting through the middle of the city carried on to wilds beyond. Those would be the destinations of my day trips out of the city. Chris had been right — if I'd given myself a full day in Inverness rather that just that afternoon and evening, I would've run out of things to do. That said, Inverness is a must-visit in Scotland, because it's a wonderful base camp.

I returned to my hotel to get some rest before an early start in the morning. The Winged Isle awaited.

The Fairy Glen, Isle of Skye

The Isle of Skye
Realm Beyond the Mist

Whilst laying in bed in the Old Tram House in Stirling, I'd made the excellent decision to add another destination to my trip. The Isle of Skye is fabled in songs and tourist pamphlets alike as one of the most breathtaking locales in the British Isles, and as I'd been told, the best that Scotland has to offer.

There are a number of tours you can book to take you there from Inverness. I picked one nearly at random with very little research before hand, given the short time in advance I'd planned the excursion. The important part is that any of them would get me there. For reasons I won't get into until later in the chapter, I won't be naming the particular tour I chose or recommending it — but do your research, and I'm sure you'll have a good time.

Before leaving, I had breakfast down in the Redcliffe Hotel's dining area. The same friendly woman who'd checked me in at the front desk was there to seat me and take my order. At the table next to me were an American and Scottish businessman going over some type of deal that he was in Inverness to close. Their back and forth reminded me of the movie *Local Hero*, wherein an American salaryman goes to Scotland on a business trip — an excellent and hilarious movie, if you've never seen it. I'd had three straight days of Full Scottish Breakfast, so I decided to take advantage of the expanded menu and have a delicious haddock omelette.

RAFFAEL CORONELLI

The tour was to meet for an early start outside another hotel on the riverfront. When I got there, I was greeted by an old English woman with a mid-sized van. The only other tour guests were an American family. It would certainly be a personal experience spending the day with these people, so I hoped they were nice.

As we drove out of Inverness, the woman — doubling as guide and driver — asked if any of us had family from Scotland. I revealed that I did, as ancestors on my mom's side come from Dingle — close to Inverness. She remarked that I was a real highlander, then, which I found amusing. She was from the north of England, not Scottish at all.

In front of us on the road as we drove past Loch Ness was a truck marked "Monster Patrol" — an obvious nod to the Loch's most famous resident. I'd be spending more time around the Loch the following day, but it certainly appeared foreboding. Before I could get a good look at it, we were moving west into more depopulated areas.

HOW TO HAVE AN ADVENTURE IN SCOTLAND

The guide said something about traffic on the road we were taking always being bad.

"I'm sure it's easier when you're having a pint," the American woman added.

Silence filled the van for a few solid seconds.

"Hopefully not while you're driving," I forced a laugh, trying to make things a little less awkward.

"Alcoholism is a very serious problem around here," the old Englishwoman scolded as she gripped the steering wheel. "We don't make light of it. I once had some tourists who'd been drinking and I wouldn't allow them back in their own car. I took their keys and called the police!"

Well, alright then. For what it's worth, I found the joke tasteless and unfunny, too. It would be an interesting day with this group, to say the least, so I tried to space out and watch the scenery out the window.

What scenery it was — rolling, green, snow-capped munros enshrouded in heavy mist surrounded us.

We were moving through the picturesque western part of the highlands toward our first real stop, a half-way point to the Isle of Skye — the intersection of Loch Duich, Loch Alsh, and Loch Long.

Left:
A sheep

103

RAFFAEL CORONELLI

Eilean Donan Castle

HOW TO HAVE AN ADVENTURE IN SCOTLAND

That compound loch, shrouded in highland mist that hangs low over the water between the surrounding munros, is the site of Eilean Donan Castle. Famous for being possibly the most picturesque castle in Scotland with its remote scenery and interesting design, it sits on a small island out in the loch, connected to the shore by a narrow stone bridge.

This design feature was intentional — if someone wanted to attack the castle, then much like the English at the Battle of Stirling Bridge, they'd be forced to cross a long, narrow passageway on which they could be easily picked off from the ramparts. This feature meant that the castle could be defended by as few as two soldiers — and indeed, two men allegedly held the fortress from a much larger attack at one point. Unfortunately, it was still vulnerable to an attack from the water, and English ships during the Jacobite Rebellion blew most of the castle to smithereens.

Rather than Stirling's seat of Scottish power, Eilean Donan was a seat of remote highland clans. Clan Mackenzie held it for most of its history. Its ruins were purchased and rebuilt by the modern descendants of Clan MacRae in the 20th century and restored to its current up-kept state.

Its private ownership unfortunately means that the castle pass I'd bought in Stirling wouldn't work here, but admission wasn't too steep.

RAFFAEL CORONELLI

Eilean Donan from the shore

Since it's technically a modern 1:1 reconstruction of a medieval castle built out of one's ruins, Eilean Donan might be the closest you can get to seeing what a place like that was actually like in its fourteenth-century prime. Tapestries hang on the walls, wood beds and tables adorn fully furnished rooms. It feels like going back to a time when it was actually in use, rather than merely visiting a historical site.

It's easy to imagine, walking through the bed chambers, what it would've been like for a member of Clan Mackenzie preparing for a visit from another clan in the great hall below.

Even the kitchen in the lower areas of the castle is equipped with pans and cooking utensils that would've been in use at the time to prepare great highland feasts.

After exploring the castle on my own, having ditched the rest of the tour party, I found my way back to the van by the time the guide had said to meet there. Then, we were off to the shore.

Eilean Donan Castle's Main Gate

Uig, Isle of Skye

HOW TO HAVE AN ADVENTURE IN SCOTLAND

Portree

The Isle of Skye is connected to the mainland by a long bridge, so it's not necessary to take the Skye boat for which the eponymous folk song was named. Still, it's hard not to hear its notes play in your mind as you look out across the water and see it — a green island, shrouded in fog, craggy green peaks and majestic cliffs overlooking the ocean.

Out the window to my right, something caught my eye on the water — several large circular metal structures dotting the Portree coastline. They were salmon farms, something you normally only hear about on a conceptual level. It was interesting to see them in Scotland, where some of the best Salmon in the world comes from.

Arriving on the island felt akin to arriving in a Celtic Lost World. This primordial landscape green of with low-hanging mist, crossed only by the road along which the van drove, gave an impression of sheer majesty.

The van stopped next to a steep incline.

"Go for a hike, half an hour," said the guide.

Go for a hike I did, in a magical place known as "the Fairy Glen." This otherworldly realm gets its name because it contains "Fairy Circles" — circular patterns in the peaty ground lined by stones. If you step into one, you may never get out, as the fairy folk will take you away. Some would actually like for that to happen — it might be preferable to the human world anyway. Still, you should keep out of them to avoid trampling these naturally occurring phenomena.

Top of the Fairy Glen

HOW TO HAVE AN ADVENTURE IN SCOTLAND

A fairy circle at the Fairy Glen

Speaking of not tampering with the Fairy Circles, you really should not move the stones around for your own purposes. Not only will you incur the wrath of supernatural beings, but of the Scots as well, not to mention my own disapproval. There's an inexplicable trend of stacking rocks on top of each other to take Instagram photos in naturalistic places. I don't know where it came from, but please refrain. If you do disturb the Fairy Circles to stack rocks, then the fairy folk will sneak into your bed during the night and eat you alive. Worse, you'll look like an embarrassing pest. Dinnae do it.

RAFFAEL CORONELLI

Climbing up a winding dirt trail, I ended up atop a great crag. Surveying the island below, wind billowed through my hair. The Isle of Skye's interesting geology caused by shifts in the land makes it look a bit different than other parts of Scotland. The colors are deep green and dark brown, earthen tones which heighten the naturalistic quality of the place differently from any other area I've visited. It's a beautiful, strange land — and that's just the visual aspect.

Inhaling the misty air, I felt like I was breathing from a cool humidifier. The perpetual fog over the island was especially low that day. On the one hand, that meant we'd be unable to see some of the more panoramic sights like the Old Man of Storr — a cliff that looks a little bit like the face of a gargantuan stone giant. On the other, it meant that the air itself was mysterious. The atmosphere over Skye carries an ancient magick — maybe not literally, but it's certainly a vibe.

Imagine, if you will, a prehistoric Scotsman arriving to this primeval world during the Stone Age and seeing the a mountain with a man's face and circles left in the ground by some unseen force. It would certainly leave an impression, considering how impressive it is in the age of Instagram.

Uig

The shifting landscape of Skye

Skye even appears in the Icelandic sagas of Nordic history. The Vikings called it the island of the cloud, referring to the perpetual fog that encompasses it. No one I've come across really knows where the name Skye comes from, but its Gaelic roots have lead to it being called "the Winged Isle" in several places like the Jethro Tull song "Acres Wild." With these varying languages and cultures feeding into its legacy, Skye is truly a place of legend.

My half-hour hike complete, I headed back to the van and converged with the rest of the party. Our next stop would be a little bit of a way across to the north end of the island — a magnificent cliff-edge vista called the Quiraing.

Up the slope of Meall na Suiramach I climbed, admittedly just a short way. Meall na Suiramach is the northern peak of the Trotternish Ridge that comprises the north tip of Skye. This all sounds very epic and cool with Gaelic names sounding like locales from *The Lord of the Rings* — not a coincidence, since Tolkien was a linguist and drew influence from these things for his own terminology. Trust me when I say that however it sounds completely represents the way it looks and feels in person.

Island of the Cloud

The Quiraing

Then, you see the Quiraing. The land drops out in front of you and you're looking to the fog-shrouded horizon. A bit of green land extends far below, dissipating into the grey North Sea. To the left and right are further peaks of the Trotternish.

Cliffs of the Trotternish

The northeast edge of Skye

Across one of those peaks was the final destination on Skye — The Mealt Falls. A plateau-top loch empties into the ocean from high above on the face of a cliff. The falls, cascading straight into the sea, resemble a moving painting of the land's end. It was the perfect cap to the majestic, awe-inspiring places I saw on the Isle of Skye.

The Mealt Falls

I'm glad that the guide was able to get me to these places and I'm grateful for that, but as I said, you need to do your research before picking a tour. I did not adequately look at reviews left by past patrons, because the Yelp page told me things I wished I'd known in hindsight about the type of conversation had in the van. Even then, I suppose it depends on the other guests.

The American family tagging along were from upstate New York. I never really hit it off with them, besides us being from the same country of origin. However, they did find common ground with the guide during the hours in which we were all stuck in that all-too-cramped van on the way back.

I don't want to complain about these things in a travel book, but ultimately, this is an anthropological observation of the culturally tumultuous period of time in which I visited. The conversation that took place between the American family and the English woman is something I will not be printing, but the manner of its content is what I can only describe as virulent and detestable.

No nationality or ethnic group were left unscathed by their derision. I was the only person in the vehicle who didn't think that immigrants to the country — even the Polish, who have been part of Inverness culture for half a millennium — were a bigger threat and taking opportunities away from Britain than the real life economic policies that devastated the city's working class.

It had left the realm of political discourse. This wasn't the strange lady in Glasgow, about which I can laugh. It was blatant vitriol, made acceptable in certain company by the Overton window shift performed by certain leaders in both of our countries.

I felt like I should've said something, but my dead silence and refusal to speak to any of them for the rest of the trip probably spoke volumes. I couldn't wait to get out of the van when we reached Inverness.

HOW TO HAVE AN ADVENTURE IN SCOTLAND

Someone reading this book will inevitably criticize me for this passage. This is an important part of the journey, though. Traveling in other countries isn't all fairy relics and beautiful vistas.

There are downsides to every culture, and what I was witnessing was a meeting of two cultures in the midst of a very specific historical period. I'm relaying to you things that some humans choose to believe, no matter what country in which you find them.

I'm also not performing a call-out in my book. All I'll do is avoid giving any names or directing anyone toward that experience. There are other ways to see the Isle of Skye.

Instead, I recommend that you take Rabbie's Isle of Skye and Eilean Donan Castle one day tour — the very same route I took. Rabbie's is a great company who showed me a wonderful time with a great guide at Loch Ness. They deserve your patronage.

I left the van behind on the streets on Inverness below the castle. It was dinner time. More importantly, I needed a strong drink.

Determined to end my day on a high note, I walked just up the street to the Castle Tavern. Inside, I found a perfect antidote to what I'd just been through — warm atmosphere, rustic decor, and ample seating.

I ordered a Lagavulin, one of the scotches that Steven's sister had recommended to me. It has a thick, peaty taste — perfect to end a day spent on the Winged Isle, and to wash away the distaste left by other things. My dinner was haggis. It was delicious, as it was the previous time I'd had it. Who'd have thought that haggis is a comfort food? It definitely is for me.

Thanks to the Castle Tavern, I was able to finish the day in a good way. I had an early night, as the next day would be another early start for another day trip.

This is what happens when you travel — you see that every country has similar ideological issues, and their inhabitants are just as susceptible to being swayed by them. The rhetoric I'd heard was vile, but it's a snapshot of a moment in time, a scene of people from two different places who'd fallen prey to the same terrible worldview.

Humans can be disheartening, but I'd met so many nice people on the trip as well. My image of Scotland was not tarnished, especially since no one in the van was actually Scottish, though I'm sure there are some Scots who would unfortunately agree with them. It just depends on the individual with whom you're interacting.

Picking apart the systemic cruelty of humanity is an unfortunate way to end my chapter about a place as magnificent as the Isle of Skye.

Luckily, there are better monsters out there. Perhaps after this train of thought, the best palette cleanser would be a good monster story — and have I got one for you.

Loch Carron

Near the Isle of Skye

Loch Ness

Loch Ness
The Black Abyss

The story goes that in some forgotten year of the Middle Ages, a peasant stole a horse from a landowner on the shore of Loch Ness. After the incident, he returned to the city with a notable physical difference — his arms now ended at the wrists. In medieval times, it was customary for rich lords to cut the hands off thieving peasants, so it would make sense for that to have been what had happened.

Instead, the peasant told a far more fantastic story.

Awaiting his punishment, he considered his situation. Hardly a fair trade, he thought, to lose one's entire dexterous ability for life because of such a comparatively inconsequential thing. The landowner had many horses, but he had only two hands. It was a fear tactic to make an example of him. That, he decided, was not to be his fate.

The peasant ran — away from the bloodthirsty landowner and down the beach. Soon he was away, free from his punishment. The sun beat down on the loch's black surface, waves lapping at his feet, mist spraying his face. He reached down and touched the water — running his fingers through it, enjoying its sensation. Whatever a fellow man had planned for him that day, his fate was now to be dealt by nature and the majesty of the highland loch.

He barely noticed the dark water beginning to churn — first further out in the loch, then moving in his direction. There was something beneath the surface, slinking closer and closer to him — something big. Its long, slender form remained hidden from view.

Waves splashed up around him, but he paid no attention. He dug his feet into the sand, oblivious, content. His enemy, as far as he was concerned, was inland. He had no idea what was coming for him.

The water exploded upward in a wall that crashed down around the peasant as he stood agape in shock. Raging toward him was the last thing he could've expected to see — a monster, bigger than any animal he'd imagined. Its mammoth head was reptilian, its teeth like broadswords.

He screamed — putting his hands up in front of him instinctively to block the onslaught of doom.

The peasant shut his eyes. He felt a sharp pain, and then the loch fell silent again. Slowly, he opened them and looked out at the peaceful waters — just as they were before the enormous, terrible creature had appeared.

His hands, however, were gone. Blood seeped from the flesh around his forearms, cleaved evenly as if with a blade.

He yelled out in despair, agony, confusion — echoing across the ominous black waters.

Perhaps this hand-eating fiend had wanted just a sampling of human flesh, a body part with lots of crunchy little bones and not a lot of succulent meat — just a nibble to satisfy its curiosity before returning to the murky abyss from whence it had risen. A larger bite would've ended the man's life instantly. This more restrained hors d'oeuvre of "finger food," so to speak, would leave him to tell of what had happened — a warning to spread to every corner of the world of what lurked under those waves.

Tavern patrons listened intently to his story of a huge monster barreling out of the waters of the loch. Was he mad? Was he lying? Did it really happen? None could tell for sure, but they all knew one thing — it was an excellent tale.

Regardless of validity, this legend persisted in obscure rumblings through the ages until the 20th century, when people started taking out-of-focus photos of rubbish floating in the water and appearing in dubious cable documentaries.

HOW TO HAVE AN ADVENTURE IN SCOTLAND

Loch Ness from Drumnadrochit

Nessie has gone from being a strange curiosity babbled about by pub drunks to an enduring pop culture icon. There's even a cartoon where she fought Godzilla. This is all thanks to Scotland's tourism industry taking full advantage of having a resident monster attraction.

The rendition you just read is indeed based on the original medieval myth of the creature as I heard it from my excellent tour guide. I wish I could tell you that I'm certain this lost legend is completely legitimate, but I cannot for the life of me find a second source. The guide had done his research very thoroughly and was regaling us with something he'd dug up. Now, I've more or less passed that story on to you, though I embellished it with a few of my own details and character beats.

Hopefully you enjoyed it, because isn't that the fun of a Loch Ness monster? A succession of tall tales that have blown up into something far more sensational than they probably were initially? When it comes down to it, that's the name of the game with Nessie — she's just an entertaining creation, and Scotland is a little bit more fun for having her.

A great thing about Nessie, and the reason the legend remains compelling, is that you can sort of pretend she's there when you look at Loch Ness. The pitch black water really could hide anything. The overcast sky, jagged munros, and smashed ruin of a castle all feel like the backdrop for an unknowable horror leftover from the depths of time. This is the biggest thing in Nessie's favor — the place in which she's said to live is extremely cool.

HOW TO HAVE AN ADVENTURE IN SCOTLAND

Seated by the same woman as before in the breakfast room, I once again ate next to the American and Scottish businessmen working out their *Local Hero* adjacent deal. I couldn't make out what exactly their business was about, but it sounded important. The uncomfortableness of the previous day was behind me, and soon I was out the door and into a Tesco to buy a bottle of Irn Bru.

As I walked next to the river with my drink, I snapped a photo and tagged the official Irn Bru Instagram account, somewhat unreasonably demanding that they sponsor me. I still haven't received that sponsorship, but we'll see how it goes after all the free publicity I'm giving their delicious, thirst-quenching, third-eye-opening beverage in this book.

Rather than outside some random hotel, the Rabbie's tour bus was set to depart from a bus terminal at the Inverness Station. Already, this was a bit more legit.

At the bus terminal were a number other tourists waiting for the tour. Among them were an older American man and his daughter about my age, and a young Northern English couple with heavy Yorkshire accents.

Soon enough, the bus pulled up and we were rolling out of the city. The guide was a very enthusiastic 30-something man with a local accent and a deep knowledge of the history of the region. Most of the good, solid information I've been giving you about Inverness is stuff I heard from him, double checked against other sources. He really knew what he was talking about.

Making things especially fun was his delivery style — unafraid of theatricality, but always coming back to facts.

Our first real destination of the tour would be Urquhart Castle. Luckily, my castle pass that I got in Stirling was good for admission, so I didn't have to pay anything extra.

RAFFAEL CORONELLI

As part of the tour, you could choose your own adventure — whether to ride the bus to the castle's land entrance, or do something more interesting — a boat ride onto the loch and to the castle. I highly recommend it despite having to pay a little more for boat tickets.

Surprisingly, only myself and the older man and his daughter were the ones who chose to go by boat. The bus pulled away, and the three of us were left to wait on the pier. Cold mist and a chilled wind blasted over the pier, billowing down over the loch from the munros above. The surface of the water stretched before us.

While waiting, I chatted with the girl who turned out to be a student at the University of Edinburgh. Her father was visiting before the start of the next semester, and they'd decided to take a trip up to the highlands. Indeed, that's a good thing to do if you're spending time in Scotland.

A great shape drew closer on the water, emerging out of the mist — a boxy, hulking form, gliding through the churning chaos of the waves with a detached elegance — a creature at home in this environment. It wasn't a monster, of course, but the boat operated by Jacobite Cruises that would take us across the way to Urquhart Castle.

We boarded and seated ourselves in the spacious interior. Screens played sonar readings of the loch below — just to see if there was anything there. Nothing showed up, but it's a fun little aspect of what amounts to a themed attraction. I opted for a more interesting view and went outside by the engines to look over the back of the boat.

Mist sprayed and wind howled — but it felt a lot more adventurous than sitting inside. Grey sky above and black water below, I held fast and took in the spectacular view.

Once you're at Loch Ness, you get the impression of how a medieval person could think a monster lived beneath. The surface of the water is, without exaggeration, a solid sheet of black. There is zero visibility below the churning waves. This leaves you to use your imagination.

Inside the sonar-equipped boat

Fear of the dark and the unknown are instinctual human survival mechanisms. Going back to the beginnings of our species evading creatures of the Pleistocene, we kept on the lookout for large predators lurking in the night beyond our campfires. Darkness can hide anything, and in the dark, there may be a monster. This is the power of Loch Ness. It's all fun at this point, but remember to keep your delicious hands inside the boat — just in case.

As per an interesting May 2018 article on Jacobite.co.uk (the cruise company's blog), some have speculated that the modern trend of people "finding" evidence of Nessie was inspired by a scene in the 1933 *King Kong* wherein a sauropod dinosaur emerges from a swamp. This certainly makes sense, as the movie was released only months prior to the famously fabricated photo that launched a million monster hunters to the loch. The folklore of Nessie had been little more than an obscure local legend before that, which I personally find more interesting; but as a monster movie fan, I have to appreciate that someone saw *King Kong* and immediately decided to look for a Scottish version.

RAFFAEL CORONELLI

Urquhart Castle from the loch

Fog parted just enough to get a glimpse of the shore to which we headed. On it was a castle — or what was left of one. Urquhart is a ruin in the most direct sense — a series of broken walls and the remains of a few towers, left this way rather unceremoniously by abandonment in the 17th century after it failed to be of use to Cromwell in his overtaking of Scotland. Despite this unremarkable end to a fortress that had stood since the first millennium A.D., Urquhart is a romantic looking ruin on the shore of a magnificent loch, adding to the eerie, haunting quality to the scenery.

Loch Ness through the remains of Urquhart Castle

RAFFAEL CORONELLI

Urquhart's ruin at the loch

HOW TO HAVE AN ADVENTURE IN SCOTLAND

It's not hard to think of a more exciting, fictional reason for the castle to be this way. If you'll indulge me for a page, I'd like to imagine such a scenario in which an English army took refuge in Urquhart on their way up to Inverness during Cromwell's conquest of the region.

The night watchman was the only member of the battalion still awake, taking refuge under the lochside wall from sheets of freezing rain. The path up to the castle from the dock was not heavily fortified. The Scots wouldn't dare attack by boat after their defeats to the south. It was like any other night in the midst of a raging highland thunderstorm.

The castle slept, aside from a few riflemen stationed on the land-facing battlements. Land was the only way a possible Scottish attack could come. The loch was too dangerous at night, too rough in the thundering rain.

Out of the black water, eyes scanned the fortress. Too long had these men fought their wars on a shore ruled by an unseen specter — one that'd now had enough.

A sound brought the watchman to attention — a splash and a thud, like a large boulder falling off the hillside and into the loch. Covering his head with his jacket, he peered out at the empty water. No boats. No enemy.

Ready to head back in from the rain, he noticed a shape move into view. It blotted out the already dark loch, made visible only by raindrops pelting its surface. The size of the castle itself, it looked like a munro had emerged from the water — with eyes, glaring down at him. Jaws opened to reveal broadsword-length teeth. He knew then that there was no time to sound the alarm — no time to get the riflemen to the opposite side of the castle — no time to comprehend this great devil that stood before him. All that remained were his final moments as teeth closed around him.

Walls shattered. Men fell into the mouth of the raging beast. Defenses facing in the wrong direction, the order was given to abandon the castle to the behemoth thrashing about the crumbling ruin. That would be the end of Urquhart.

I want to reiterate that this didn't actually happen. Like that handless medieval peasant, I simply enjoy monster stories. By all means, visit Loch Ness and tell your own Nessie stories, because it's a tradition that should continue.

The boat lets you out at the aforementioned path up from the dock. From there, you can enter the ruin on the lower level, where you'll find a museum exhibit. Then, you'll ascend into the ruin.

Cool wind blew off the loch and over the broken walls — the very same force that had toppled them. Despite surviving centuries of warfare amongst humankind, the only things that could demolish the castle after its historical abandonment were the elements of the loch itself.

Only two parts of the ruin remain intact enough to provide any real remnant of its full architecture — part of a battlement, which you can climb atop, and a single tower, which you can go inside and ascend its spiral stair. The tower provides a romantic view of the loch.

On the way up to the car park, I passed a full-scale trebuchet replica set up on the castle grounds from which a land attack would have come. It wasn't the Warwolf, but it was still impressive to see the 30-foot siege engine up close.

The full-scale trebuchet at Urquhart Castle

Locks at the Caledonian Canal's entrance to Loch Ness

HOW TO HAVE AN ADVENTURE IN SCOTLAND

While waiting for the bus to return, I chatted a little bit with the Yorkshire couple. I'd visited Yorkshire when I was about two and a half years old, so I only had the vaguest of memories of it, but they were lovely people and were enjoying their holiday in Scotland.

Back on the bus, we circled around the loch, the guide giving more excellent information on Inverness and the surrounding area. Our next stop was the town at the bottom of the loch, Fort Augustus — both for lunch, and for a little bit of a walk around the town.

After eating in a pub, I walked down the to see the locks that let water in to the loch. This isn't a play on words — there are literally locks that raise and lower the level of the water to allow boats in and out of Loch Ness via the Caledonian Canal. The locks were under construction at the time so I didn't see them in action, but they were impressive.

More impressive was the view from the bottom of Loch Ness. Getting down next to the water, I watched the sunlight glinting off its dark surface. Monster aside, the loch is just a beautiful place to take in, both on an aesthetic level and in the serenity it gives off.

Back on the bus, the guide told the story of the original myth that I relayed at the beginning of this chapter, along with another interesting factoid that adds to the loch's eeriness. One Alister Crowley once lived on its shore, practicing his black magicks. The guide told of how Crowley was part of the British war effort during World War II as he attempted to develop spells to counter what he feared was Hitler's use of the occult. Again, I don't believe in that sort of thing, but its vibe definitely goes with the atmosphere. Imagine Nessie in the water, a dark conjurer on land, mists of the munros swirling as thunder clapped around them. Loch Ness is exactly the type of environment where one can picture such a thing.

The Nessie Hunter

One of the final stops of the tour was a spot on the beach overlooking the loch. The sun was getting lower in the late afternoon sky. Just before the sand was an RV, parked in a permanent spot.

"I always bring the tourists to him," said the guide. "I like to give him the business."

The RV belonged to the Nessie Hunter — an eccentric local who lives on the shore of the loch and makes handmade ceramic Nessie trinkets.

His reason for being there is that, years ago, he saw Nessie herself. I don't want to discredit a man's life's work, I just find it fascinating to look at someone so singularly driven by one thing.

After meeting him, I am absolutely convinced that he believes he saw Nessie. In his mind, he really did see the monster, and he came to Loch Ness to spend his life and livelihood trying to get another glimpse.

HOW TO HAVE AN ADVENTURE IN SCOTLAND

Day in and day out, he sells his wares to busses full of tourists, all the while keeping an eye on the loch from his RV — waiting. Someday, he thinks, she'll rise up before him.

He's not harming anyone, at least not that I'm aware. He's making his little souvenirs and providing entertainment to tourists. Still — he really believes, and waits for the day he'll see the monster again.

Maybe, on his final day, she'll appear before him and take him down into the water. Maybe it won't happen at all. The Nessie Hunter is a unique person living a unique life in a unique place, a harmless and colorful character with a singular purpose.

I bought a little Nessie statuette from him. It's well made, and has a personal touch that you won't get from assembly-line gift shop items. If you come across the Nessie Hunter's shop, definitely pick one up. After all, it's sculpted from memory.

A ceramic Nessie sculpted by the Nessie Hunter
now in the author's collection

RAFFAEL CORONELLI

The black waters of Loch Ness and the descending sun

The tour bus dropped us back off at the station. I said goodbye to the guide and thanked him for the extremely informative tour. Then, I bid farewell to the other guests, and walked up the street to my new regular dinner spot in Inverness, the Castle Tavern.

I'd had a fantastic day, so I was in a much better mood walking in than I was the previous night. I sat at the bar this time, and pulled up my list of remaining Scotches that I wanted to try. The first I asked the bartender for was Glenfarclas.

Searching the bar behind her, she soon realized it wasn't there. I was about to move on to the next Scotch on my list when she called over another bartender.

"Do we have Glenfarclas?" she asked him.

"Aye," he answered, "it's downstairs."

"Well, go get it."

"You don't have to do all that just for me," I laughed.

"Oh it's no trouble," she replied.

Haggis Cigars at the Castle Tavern

Glenfarclas was another good one, not quite as peaty but smooth and delicious. That list of recommended Scotches never failed me. My second drink to go with dinner was a Laphroaig, which I'd had at the wedding. Dinner was "haggis cigars" — haggis shaped into little rolls that you can eat like sausage links with crunchy outer shells that hold their shape. They were delicious, as haggis always is.

This was my final night in Inverness. I'd be leaving without a monster sighting, but the wealth of experience more than made up for it. What a place, Loch Ness is. Keep an eye on the dark water, and keep your hands to yourself. You never know who might be hungry.

The Castle Tavern bustled with locals. I took an earthy, peaty sip of my Laphroaig and chomped into a haggis cigar with a monstrous crunch.

Edinburgh's Old Town and Calton Hill from Edinburgh Castle

Edinburgh
Medieval Metropolis

"This is your holiday," said the woman who'd previously served me breakfast every morning as she checked me out at the front desk, apparently in surprise.

Maybe she'd thought I was somehow part of the business meeting that had been conducted over breakfast the last two days.

In the train station, also waiting for the southbound line, I sat down next to two familiar faces — the man and his daughter from the previous day's Loch Ness tour. They were perfectly friendly once again, and I exchanged pleasantries with them until it was time to board. My ticket's assigned seat took me away from them, so I never really got to properly see them off, but I'm sure they made it back to Edinburgh alright.

Unlike the trip up from Stirling, there would be no changing trains. Inverness to Edinburgh is a straight shot, one that'll take you a good portion of the day. Gazing out the window, I said goodbye to the highlands — majestic peaks and winding rivers fading away into shorter hills and open glens. The Pass of Drumochter vanished behind us, and we were in the lowlands once again.

Then the buildings grew tighter, bigger — more so than they'd been anywhere since Glasgow. An urban area overtook the train, and with it, I knew we'd entered Scotland's capital and largest city.

Edinburgh is easily Scotland's most visited location for foreign tourists, and there's a good reason for that. The city itself is stunning, and has so much to do — the Tokyo of Scotland, if you will.

My hotel was the Kimpton Charlotte Square — the swankiest (and most expensive) place I stayed the whole trip. All things considered for the quality of the accommodations and its central location, it was still a great deal and would heartily recommend it if you don't mind a little bit of a splurge in a city that makes you feel like that's what you should be doing.

The Kimpton felt more continental European than traditionally Scottish like the last few places I stayed. That fits Edinburgh's character as an international city, Scotland's gateway to England to the immediate south, and to the rest of the world. That isn't to say that Edinburgh doesn't feel Scottish — it certainly does, and it contains a host of things that you'll see nowhere else — but it's a little bit more accessible and global than someplace like Inverness, or even the rough-and-tumble charm of Glasgow.

Charlotte Square itself is a little bit of a walk from the station, and is an impressive collection of architecture to take in. Its centerpiece is the Albert Memorial statue, depicting Victoria's husband Prince Albert on horseback. On the west side looms the magnificent green dome of the West Register House, an architecturally impressive government building.

HOW TO HAVE AN ADVENTURE IN SCOTLAND

Travel had taken up the majority of my day. As I checked in to my room, the sun was already beginning to set, and I was ready to look for a good pub to get some nourishment and finish out my list of recommended Scotches — and maybe, since I was feeling a little adventurous, talk to some of the locals.

Edinburgh has had a few literary connections throughout its history, but I have a personal favorite — Robert Louis Stevenson's The Strange Case of Doctor Jekyll and Mister Hyde. Deacon Brodie's Tavern in the Old Town section of Edinburgh (more on the differentiation between Old and New Town a little bit later) is the still-running, centuries-old pub where Deacon Brodie frequented. Brodie was the inspiration for Stevenson, who lived in Edinburgh, to invent the character of Dr. Jekyll and his dual persona. There wasn't an elixir or a transformation involved with the real man, but it's still a must-see for those with an interest in monsters, horror, literature, or violence. I never got a chance to drink there as it was always obscenely crowded, but I'm happy to say that I saw the outside of it, at least.

As I slunk out of my hotel on Charlotte Square to roam the backstreets of New Town Edinburgh, I probably resembled the creeping, fiendish Hyde prowling for the next victim of his senseless brutality. In actuality, I was just looking for a drink and some form of haggis.

The first pub I encountered was far too crowded. All pubs in Edinburgh are always crowded, but this was ridiculous — I couldn't even get close to the bar. Dejected, I moved on to the next one.

The next pub didn't have quite as obscene an amount of patrons, allowing me to grab a seat. Immediately, I asked the bar tender if he had Ardbeg — the one scotch recommended to me that I hadn't yet tried. He happily informed me that they did, and poured me a glass of rich, smooth, complex flavored scotch.

Ardbeg is absolutely top-notch. It doesn't have quite the extreme peat-eating experience that my top favorite Scotches deliver, but its nuanced taste definitely makes up for it. If you don't love the flavor of peat as much as I do, it may very well be the best Scotch you'll find.

For my food item, I ordered a plate of haggis balls. These were bite-sized balls made out of — well, you know.

Locals started leaning in over my shoulder to place their orders with the bar tender. A middle-aged man with a northern English accent ordered something, apologizing for leaning on me while he did it. I told him it was alright and laughed, taking him aback.

"You're from America?" he said, incredulous. "What are you doing here?"

I don't know, what are *you* doing here?

Rather than say that out loud, I told him I was on a trip after going to my friend's wedding. He talked to me for a little bit, mostly about how he and his mates come up over the border to Edinburgh on weekends. It was Friday night, which was why the place was so crowded. He went back to his mates, the gang of middle-aged northern English blokes having drinks together. He'd been well meaning, if a little coarse, but it was a memorable interaction.

HOW TO HAVE AN ADVENTURE IN SCOTLAND

Realizing I'd finished my Ardbeg, I asked the bartender for a recommendation. Smiling, he pulled down a bottle with a blue label inscribed "Kilchoman". This, he explained, was from a distillery in Islay, where the peatiest scotch (including Laphroaig) is made. Kilchoman, I later learned, is not available in the United States. I could be wrong — if you can find it, please let me know! The bar tender said it was his personal favorite scotch, and seeing that my tastes and his were aligning, I agreed to have a glass.

Suddenly, I was no longer in the crowded pub. I was on top of a green munro, looking out to the misty horizon. Smokey peat rolled over my tongue like the rolling hills of the western Highlands. This was the best Scotch I'd had.

"Oh, it's delicious," I said to the bar tender, who smiled in approval.

That was when my peaty serenity was interrupted by three young English guys ordering beers over my shoulder. They were all about twenty and seemed oblivious to my presence, but I figured I might as well say something.

"Hi!" I introduced myself.

"You're from America?" the one closest to me said immediately.

"Yeah, I was visiting some friends in Glasgow."

"What are you doing in Edinburgh?"

"Having fun," I said, to which they laughed.

"Yeah," I continued, "I was just up in Inverness."

"Inverness," they laughed amongst each other in what sounded like an imitation of a South African accent — no idea if they were failing to imitate my own Chicago accent or a Highland Scots one, but either would've been wildly off the mark.

They were from England — not northern England like the middle aged guys who'd just come over the border, but from further south with a more London-sounding accent.

"What do you do?" asked one of them.

"A few things," I said. "I'm a writer. I have a few books out."

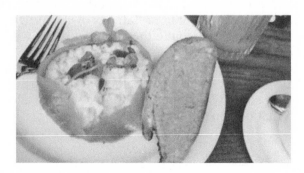

"You've gotta tell people that," he said, obviously a little drunk already. "Like, you're obviously not gonna be J.R.R. Tolkien, but keep at it."

"For sure," I laughed at getting life advise from a drunk person several years my junior.

The rowdy English lads eventually left to go get something at their hotel, and I was left on my own in the bar — two scotches deep and a little exhausted from the day's journey. I wasn't going anywhere else that night, so I closed out the tab and headed back to Charlotte Square.

Back in the room, I turned on the BBC. It was the day the UK government had planned for Brexit to go through, but parliament once again kicked it down the road after indecision. Tumultuous times were ahead, but more imminently, I had two full days to explore Edinburgh — and that would require getting some rest first.

The Kimpton's opulent breakfast room, or rather indoor courtyard, was a wonderful place to begin my first full day in the city. Sunlight filtered in through skylights onto my table as a French-accented waiter took my order for a Scottish salmon omelette.

Edinburgh Castle looms over the New Town

RAFFAEL CORONELLI

Ross Fountain

HOW TO HAVE AN ADVENTURE IN SCOTLAND

My first stop of the day would be the eponymous Edinburgh Castle. I'd seen it looming over George Street when I'd come in to the station (it's hard to miss), but I was looking forward to actually going up and seeing it. It was my final castle of the trip, and the last place to use the pass I'd gotten in Stirling.

The park in front of the castle is home to the Ross Fountain, named for its historical owner who erected it in Edinburgh in the mid-19th century. With the backdrop of the castle, it's a remarkable sight.

Edinburgh Castle itself sits atop a great slab of rock above the city that's fittingly called Castle Rock — the extinct caldera of a long-silent volcano. The castle itself is Edinburgh's oldest settlement, and while it doesn't quite have the turbulent strategic importance of Stirling, its position in the heart of Scotland's southern capital makes it one of the most prominent historical fortresses in the country (and by far the most frequently visited).

Edinburgh Castle ramparts from the side of Castle Rock

Edinburgh Castle esplanade

The are a few striking similarities between the experiences of visiting Edinburgh and Stirling Castles. For one, they're fully intact, rebuilt from any past destruction they've endured — not quite the period restoration of Eilean Donan, but a far cry from the windswept ruins of Urquhart. For another, they're situated strategically at the top of great pinnacles — though Edinburgh's uneven landscape and layers of building since the Middle Ages has lead to a multi-level metropolis that reaches Castle Rock's height in a few other places, somewhat diminishing its absolute dominance over the skyline.

The castle wall with Edinburgh's New Town below

Edinburgh Castle's Middle Ward

That isn't to say in the least that Edinburgh Castle isn't impressive. Its thick walls and sprawling layout cover the top of Castle Rock like a man made extension of the rock itself. Perched on its mount, it watches over the dense metropolis from above — and the view of the city from the castle is an interesting contrast of architectural styles.

The New Town from the top of Edinburgh Castle

RAFFAEL CORONELLI

A cannon battery overlooks the New Town

The One O'Clock Gun

If you have any interest in artillery, Edinburgh Castle is home to an assortment that will delight you. Mons Meg is a medieval super weapon with a twenty-inch barrel, weighing more than six and a half tonnes. This wide, squat cannon is imposing in person, long after its actual use. One can only imagine the carnage that would ensue on the receiving end of its horrific blast.

Less outwardly violent in use is the One O'Clock Gun — a British artillery cannon that is fired once a day to help Edinburgh keep the time. It was only used in combat once, when a German zeppelin flew over Edinburgh during a First World War air raid and the cannon fired at it. I'll let you guess what time the One O'Clock Gun is fired, in case you want to hear it go off.

RAFFAEL CORONELLI

Edinburgh Castle is also home to the Crown Jewels of Scotland, and the Stone of Destiny, on which ancient Scottish rulers were coronated. These are an immensely popular and crowded attraction, but the line moves quickly enough. The only downside is that you move right through without getting a good chance to stop and see them very closely. Your mileage will vary based on how much you want to see these and whether dealing with the crowd is worth it.

The Castle has so much to do that it'll easily take up half of your day. The other half of my day would be spent just across the bridge in the Old Town.

Edinburgh is divided in two. The New Town was built in the Georgian era, and has an opulent architecture typified by Charlotte Square, where I was staying. The Old Town dates back to the Middle Ages.

Because of the uneven terrain, Old Town is on higher ground than New Town — but there's an even more interesting reason for the medieval city being raised up on what appears to be a higher level. The original, Black Death-era city is literally underneath the streets of the current one. Underfoot of those who walk the Royal Mile and its adjacent closes (connecting alleys), a whole different system of streets runs beyond the reach of daylight — centuries out of use, buried forever with ghosts of a darker time.

There is a way of touring this lost subterranean realm, and it's the attraction I most highly recommend out of anything in the Old Town — Mary King's Close.

To get there, you need to walk the aforementioned Royal Mile, which is an attraction unto itself. Stretching from the castle to Holyrood Abbey, the mile of road is lined by glorious medieval architecture. A bagpipe player serenaded people on the street as I walked past, and a strange looking monster mascot waved to tourists. It feels a bit theme park adjacent at times, but it's all great fun — and there's nothing phony about it. Old Town is a real deal medieval city that engulfs you, waiting to pull you down into its murky depths.

HOW TO HAVE AN ADVENTURE IN SCOTLAND

The Royal Mile

RAFFAEL CORONELLI

A narrow close in Edinburgh's Old Town

HOW TO HAVE AN ADVENTURE IN SCOTLAND

Once you buy your ticket to Mary King's Close, you can walk the surrounding area until it's time for your tour. The aforementioned Deacon Brodie's Tavern is nearby, though as I said, it was too crowded to even get inside.

The guide taking the group and I down into Mary King's Close was a twenty-something actress dressed in a medieval costume. That might sound theme park-adjacent like I said before, but she really knew her stuff and gave a great, atmospheric tour.

Mary King's Close was a market street underneath the Royal Mile in the early medieval era of the city. Now, it's entirely built over, a sunless realm unchanged since the time when the Black Death ravaged the city.

Houses in which people lived, streets where people walked, and an incredible depth of history await in this underground realm. It was one of my favorite things I did in Edinburgh, and I can't recommend it highly enough. When it was over and we headed back up to the surface, I thanked the guide for the wonderful time I'd had.

Having done a certain amount of medieval exploration, there was one more thing I needed to address that day — I was about to run out of clean underwear. To remedy this, I headed to Primark on Princes Street, where I bought some new undergarments. Despite not having had time for laundry, I wouldn't stink up Scotland for my final two days.

My last day in Edinburgh began once again in the sunlit breakfast room at the Kimpton. This time, I ordered the Full Scottish Breakfast — black pudding, white pudding, sausage, the works. As always, it was immensely satisfying.

The castle and Mary King's Close were the two attractions I'd most intently planned on visiting, so I thought I'd take my second day to visit an assortment of other places I hadn't considered too closely.

The first was the Scott Monument on Princes Street. This centrally located spire is impossible to miss in Edinburgh, but it's worth seeing up close. Looking up at the sky-piercing, gothic, ornate monument to Sir Walter Scott gives one a sense of pure awe. I wasn't able to go up into it as it was closed at the time, but you can check to see if that's possible when you visit.

The Scott Monument

HOW TO HAVE AN ADVENTURE IN SCOTLAND

Arthur's Seat from the top of Nelson Monument

Open for climbing was the Nelson Monument, atop Calton Hill. The height of the more than 100-foot castle-like tower is amplified more than five and a half times by the hill on which it sits, making it the best possible vantage point from which to see Edinburgh. There's one catch — you have to walk up 142 steps in the incredibly steep, winding spiral staircase inside the tower.

As soon as I stepped out onto the tower's balcony, I forgot all about the strenuous climb. Edinburgh spread out below. To the south was Arthur's Seat — a great mountain that overlooks the city. To the west was the New Town, Charlotte Square, the castle, and Old Town beyond it.

Old and New Town visible from the Nelson Monument

RAFFAEL CORONELLI

Aside from the Nelson Monument, I spent about an hour walking around the top of Calton Hill, which is home to a number of other attractions like the observatory and the National Monument of Scotland. These were nice to see, and all part of the open-air reprieve from the dense city below.

There were two things left on my agenda for the afternoon, both of them museums. National museums in Scotland are free, which is something you should absolutely take advantage of. The first I visited was the Scottish National Gallery, a museum of fine art with fantastic pieces.

The second was the National Museum of Scotland. This has everything from cultural artifacts to prehistoric skeletons. It also has an extremely ornate clock representing the horrors of the second millennium A.D. called the Millennium Clock Tower, which goes off and does a musical number several times a day. Apparently the schedule changes, but I was lucky enough to see it happen. The museum is free, so go in and have a look.

Right:
The Millennium Clock
at the National Museum of
Scotland

HOW TO HAVE AN ADVENTURE IN SCOTLAND

After the museum, I needed to find dinner. It was time for some cheeky Nando's.

I am absolutely baffled by Nando's. British people consider it fast food, but you have to sit down and have someone bring you your order. It feels more like "fast casual" to me, except you order at a counter. I found going in and placing my order to be a strange and confounding experience that I had to figure out as I was doing it. I got some kind of spicy chicken sandwich, which was pretty good, but I still find Nando's incomprehensible on a conceptual level. Cheeky Nando's, indeed!

There's so much to do in the city of Edinburgh that you'll inevitably exhaust yourself by the end of your stay. Two days wasn't enough to see it all, but I really crammed my two days full of activity — both physical and intellectual. Ultimately, you can see why Edinburgh is spoken of so highly by everyone who visits. I might personally prefer the character of Glasgow, but Edinburgh is an overwhelming experience that you must have — and can only have in Scotland's medieval theme park of a capital city.

The Equestrian Statue of the Duke of Wellington
with matching hats

Return to Glasgow
The High Road

A strange feeling took me as I stepped onto George Square for the first time in over two weeks. It felt like I was returning home to a city in which I'd spent only two days. There are a handful cities scattered across the globe that give me this feeling of returning to a welcome and familiar place, full of a hardy character with which I can identify. Glasgow is among them.

After taking in George Square for a moment, I headed up Queen Street and passed the Equestrian Duke of Wellington statue. This time, both he and his horse were wearing matching traffic cones on their heads. One has to respect a man who coordinates his hat with his horse's.

Descending into the subway, I took the train a few stops to a familiar location — the West End neighborhood where my friends had lead me around to the pubs. This was where my hotel was located — just down B808 from the castle-like tower of Oran Mor. Passing by the place in the daytime had a different vibe, but it looked just as impressive.

My accommodation for the final night in Scotland was the Belhaven Hotel (no relation to the brewery). A Victorian era building, the hotel was comfortable and convenient enough for my one-night stay, and gave me a real sense of Glaswegian atmosphere with its high ceilings and winding staircase. Most importantly, it would allow me to spend my last day in Scotland exploring a part of Glasgow that I'd only visited at night.

RAFFAEL CORONELLI

A light mist and drizzle of rain fell as I walked down B808 — not enough to warrant an umbrella but enough to make one's clothes slightly damp. It was the perfect day for visiting one of Glasgow's West End daytime attractions, the Glasgow Botanic Garden.

Walking the grounds of the botanic garden gave me one last jolt of Scottish greenery. Standing at the edge of a river, I took a deep breath of cool, misty air.

Rain started to come down a bit harder, so I decided to go inside and see the main attraction of the gardens. Kibble Palace is an architecturally pleasing 19th century wrought-iron glasshouse filled with all manner of beautiful tropical plants — some one which are carnivorous and crave the sweet taste of flesh. It's a great place to get inside from the cold, damp Scottish weather and take in some humidity and pure, oxygen-rich air straight from the source.

Other greenhouses on the premises contain an array of warm weather plants and a few animals, like a small fish pond I came across. It was the perfect way to spend a rainy early afternoon.

Kibble Palace

Interior of Kibble Palace at Glasgow Botanic Garden

Oran Mor

HOW TO HAVE AN ADVENTURE IN SCOTLAND

Having seen the gardens, I headed out into the chilly West End to get something for an early dinner. I'd be meeting my Glaswegian friends from the wedding for one last drink at Oran Mor that night, but I wanted to eat something first. I'd had Scottish pub food nearly every day for the last two and a half weeks — so I decided it was time to sample some of Glasgow's wide array of cuisine brought by its vibrant immigrant population.

Passing a Vietnamese restaurant called Non Viet Hai, I decided that would be my choice. A noodle soup is the perfect way to warm up after walking around in the cold rain. Entering, I was seated in the well decorated interior by a single waiter. I ordered bun bo hue, a spicy noodle soup similar to pho.

The food arrived, and I dug in. It was, without exaggeration, possibly the spiciest thing I've ever eaten. Tears literally ran down my cheeks and dropped into the soup, just like my quickly ending time in Scotland. It was delicious, but extremely spicy. I would recommend it with a warning. Otherwise, just get regular pho, which I'm sure is great at such a high quality and authentic restaurant.

Night arrived, and with it, I made my way back to Oran Mor. The dark tower of my favorite Glasgow pub lit up with a purple spotlight at the end of the street — a majestic sight, and a fine destination for my final night.

My friends were already waiting for me inside. I grabbed a pint of Belhaven brown ale and sat with them in a corner of the medieval-atmosphered tavern. They asked about my trip, and I regaled them with my stories much as I have to you. I asked the American expat what the process of immigrating into Scotland was like, which sounded like an interesting ordeal.

It was a lovely final evening with my friends. I didn't want to go, but all things end eventually. Resigned we must be while we're parting. Of course, I promised that I'd be back — a promise I intend to keep.

The next day, I awoke and headed downstairs bright and early to have my final Full Scottish Breakfast at the Belhaven. Despite the time drawing near when I'd have to leave, I enjoyed each sausage link, each bloodthirsty bite of black pudding, each roasted tomato. My final meal in Scotland couldn't have been more fitting.

I took a cab to the airport with barely enough time to spare to get to the gate. Seated on the plane to London before takeoff, I looked out at the city.

Scotland had been an adventure — not in the trite sense that one uses to describe going anywhere, but an actual adventure on which I'd experienced things I could never have planned, met people with whom I'd stay in touch, and gotten the full experience of the culture from the inside. It was the best the trip could have gone.

It was also something of an encapsulation of a specific point in time. You can retrace my steps, and I encourage you to do so. However, I'd taken the trip at a crossroads, a moment that will never come again.

Before the plague and turmoil that engulfed the world the following year — before another trip of even grander ambition through the north of Japan, about which I've also written a book — I'd spent two and a half weeks in Scotland that I'd never forget.

Maybe, like all the wars and horrors of times past embedded in castle ruins, the darkness of today will pass like a gust of wind on the Quiraing, dissipating like mist over a highland loch. Maybe, when we all meet in Scotland again, it'll be a better day for all.

The plane rumbled and left Glasgow below, ascending into the low-hanging clouds from whence it emerged — taking the high road as Scotland took the low road.

North Gate of Stirling Castle

RAFFAEL CORONELLI

A Glencairn style scotch glass

HOW TO HAVE AN ADVENTURE IN SCOTLAND

SCOTCHES TO DRINK IN SCOTLAND
(OR ELSEWHERE)

Laphroaig
Peaty, smoky, transportive, this is a relentless scotch that'll hit you like highland wind rolling off a munro.

Lagavulin
A bit less intense in its peat levels, but no less flavor. Smoky and smooth.

Glenfarclas
Very smooth, and surprisingly affordable for such a high quality distillery. A good entry level single malt that remains a favorite.

Ardbeg
Complex, thick, layered taste that changes as it rolls across your tongue. Lots of different flavors going on in every sip.

Kilchoman
Islay peat extravaganza. Drink this one in Scotland, but let me know if you can find it overseas. The Edinburgh bartender's choice.

Raffael Coronelli is a Chicago-based world adventurer and writer of novels, scripts, and other pieces. His works include the *How to Have an Adventure in...* travel book series, the *Daikaiju Yuki* novel series, an audio drama for the Kaijusaurus Podcast, and essays for blu-ray releases from Arrow Video.

Follow:

@RAFFLEUPAGUS

daikaijuyuki.com/raffael-coronelli

More adventures:

Ten cities and towns from Hokkaido to Tokyo.
Author Raffael Coronelli invites you on an adventure through
Northern Japan's ancient mountain temples and frozen
metropolises — journeying into local culture and cuisine, Beautiful
locales, pop culture touchstones, Japan-only establishments, and
meeting all the people along the way.

From midnight sunlit fjords to the eccentric fun of Scandinavian cities — a two-plus week journey through Norway, into the arctic, and back down to Denmark. Author Raffael Coronelli invites you on a Nordic saga through breathtaking landscapes and legends, with knowledge straight from locals and travel tips. Culinary delicacies, extreme pop culture, Vikings, and Scandinavian beauty await.

It all started with some beers.

A party at sea. What could go wrong? A deadly attack by vile pirates working in tandem with horrific creatures leaves the surviving revelers imprisoned on their way to a secret cove and an unknown destiny. What will they find when they get there? Is there any hope to survive their tyrannical captors?

Who, or what, is the Pharaoh of Eels?

Available as an illustrated novella
and an audiobook read by Steven Sloss.

Squirreled away in the mists of Scotland lies the town of Dunwith, where a strange community of people live freely in splendid isolation. The town only appears to the outside world for one day each year, which is celebrated locally as *Dunwith Day*.

VISIT DUNWITH TODAY

searchword: "dunwithTV"